A. Gol 795

The Fourteen Stations of the Cross

A Suite for Organ

Alan Ridout

Kevin Mayhew

We hope you enjoy *The Fourteen Stations of the Cross*.
Further copies are available from your local
music shop or Christian bookshop.

In case of difficulty, please contact the publisher direct by writing to:

The Sales Department
KEVIN MAYHEW LTD
Rattlesden
Bury St Edmunds
Suffolk IP30 0SZ

Phone 0449 737978
Fax 0449 737834

Please ask for our complete catalogue of outstanding Church Music.

Front Cover: *The Deposition* by Bernard van Orley (c.1488-1541).
Reproduced by kind permission of Alan Jacobs Gallery, London/
Bridgeman Art Library, London.

Front cover designed by Juliette Clarke and Graham Johnstone
Picture Research: Jane Rayson

First published in Great Britain in 1994 by Kevin Mayhew Ltd

© Copyright 1994 Kevin Mayhew Ltd

ISBN 0 86209 501 8
Catalogue No: 1400014

The music in this book is protected by copyright and may not be reproduced
in any way for sale or private use without the consent of the copyright owner.

Music Setting: Tricia Oliver
Music Editor: Donald Thomson

Printed and bound in Great Britain

Contents

	Page
1. Jesus is condemned to death	4
2. Jesus receives the cross	8
3. Jesus falls the first time	10
4. Jesus meets his blessed mother	12
5. The cross is laid upon Simon of Cyrene	14
6. Veronica wipes the face of Jesus	16
7. Jesus falls the second time	18
8. Jesus speaks to the women of Jerusalem	20
9. Jesus falls the third time	22
10. Jesus is stripped of his garments	24
11. Jesus is nailed to the cross	25
12. Jesus dies on the cross	26
13. Jesus is taken down from the cross	28
14. Jesus is laid in the sepulchre	30

Composer's Note

This work was suggested by the sculptured reliefs of the Stations to be seen in the Cistercian monastic church in Altenburg, Westphalia, Germany. The music consists of thirteen variations on a theme which is heard only in its complete form when the fourteenth Station is reached.

ALAN RIDOUT

THE FOURTEEN STATIONS OF THE CROSS

Alan Ridout (*b.*1934)

1. Jesus is condemned to death

© Copyright 1994 by Kevin Mayhew Ltd.
It is illegal to photocopy music.

Attacca

2. Jesus receives the cross

3. Jesus falls the first time

4. Jesus meets his blessed mother

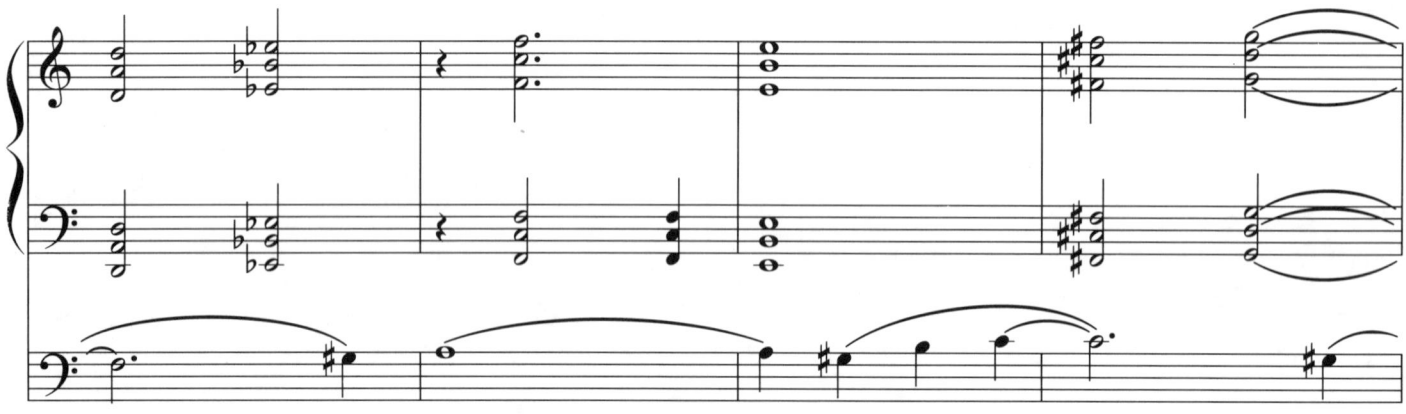
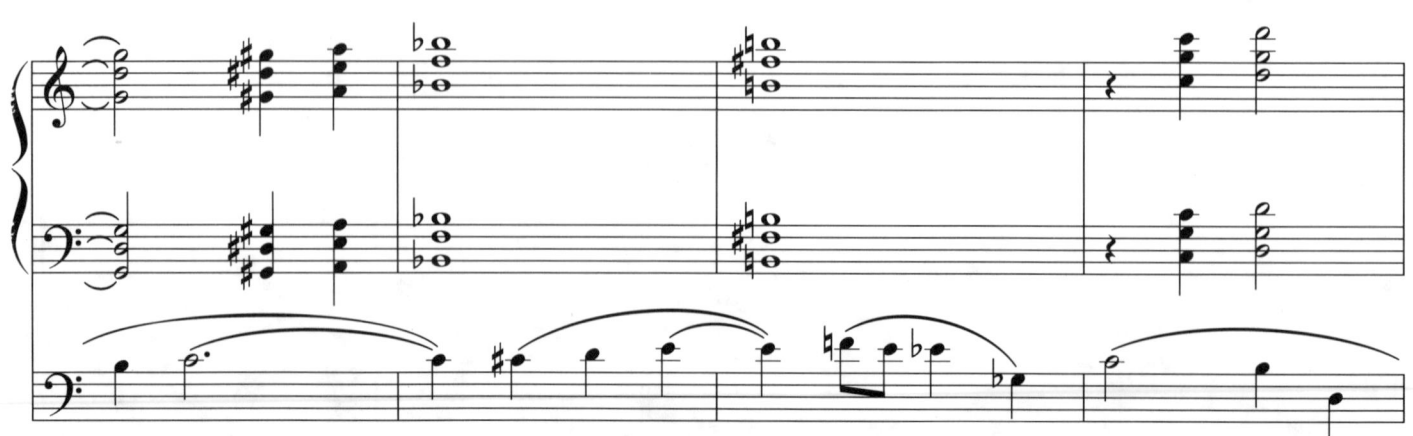

© Copyright 1994 by Kevin Mayhew Ltd.
It is illegal to photocopy music.

5. The cross is laid upon Simon of Cyrene

© Copyright 1994 by Kevin Mayhew Ltd.
It is illegal to photocopy music.

6. Veronica wipes the face of Jesus

7. Jesus falls the second time

8. Jesus speaks to the women of Jerusalem

9. Jesus falls the third time

10. Jesus is stripped of his garments

© Copyright 1994 by Kevin Mayhew Ltd.
It is illegal to photocopy music.

11. Jesus is nailed to the cross

* Chromatic clusters between the given notes

© Copyright 1994 by Kevin Mayhew Ltd.
It is illegal to photocopy music.

*As many notes as possible using hand and forearm

12. Jesus dies on the cross

Chorale (𝅗𝅥 = c.48)

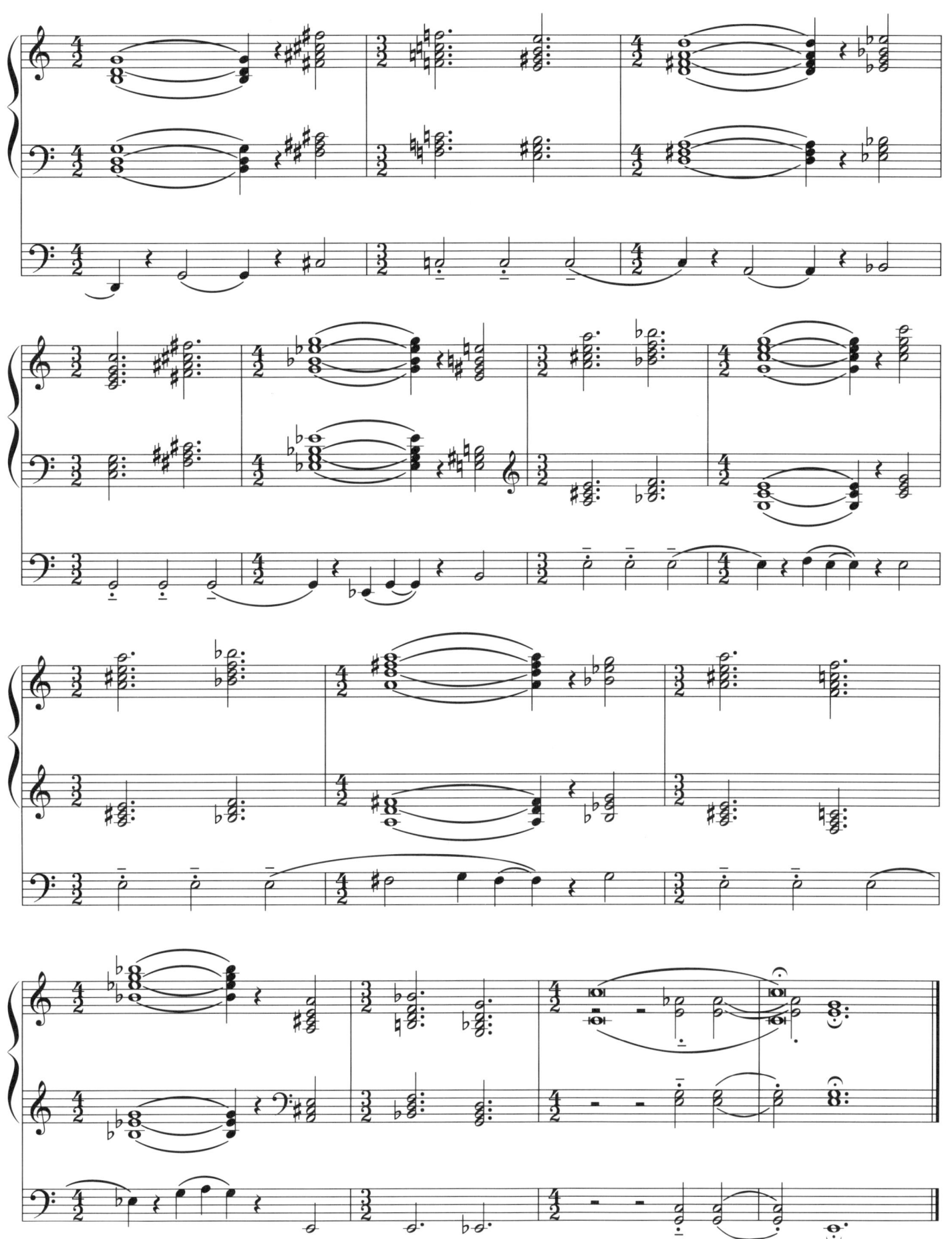

13. Jesus is taken down from the cross

© Copyright 1994 by Kevin Mayhew Ltd.
It is illegal to photocopy music.

14. Jesus is laid in the sepulchre

© Copyright 1994 by Kevin Mayhew Ltd.
It is illegal to photocopy music.

32

Collins

Edexcel GCSE 9-1
Maths Higher

Trevor Senior, Anne Stothers and Leisa Bovey

Andreas Georgiades

Exam Skills and **Practice**

How to use this book

This Exam Skills and Practice book puts the spotlight on the different types of command word - the instructional word or phrase in a question - you can expect to find in your GCSE papers. Each section has worked examples and lots of timed practice to help build your exam technique.

Top Tips offer nuggets of information to keep in mind when answering each type of question.

Scan the QR code to test your understanding of the command word and see worked solutions to the example question(s) on that page.

Each question shows the part of the specification and grade range icons show whether a calculator is allowed 🖩 or not 🚫🖩.

Complete the example to take the next step in your practice. Parts of the workings and/or answers are given for you to finish. Helpful hints also steer you in the right direction.

Each **command word** is defined in easy-to-understand language.

Example questions show the command words in context. Use the QR code to access worked video solutions and commentary for them.

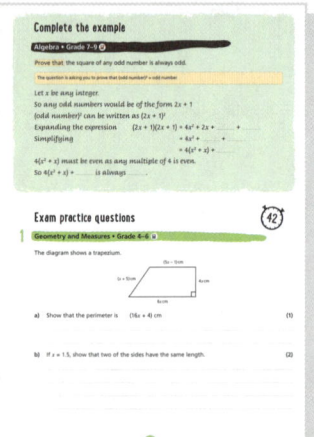

Exam practice questions enable you to delve deeper into each command word across a range of topics and grade levels. There is a target time for doing these at exam speed.

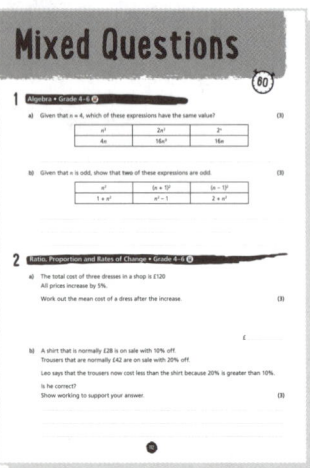

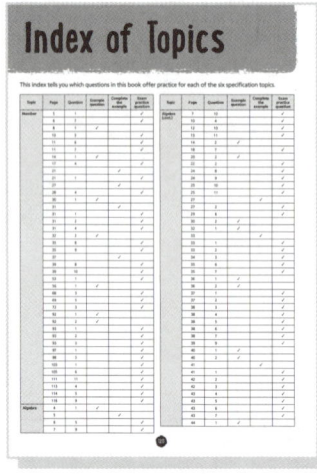

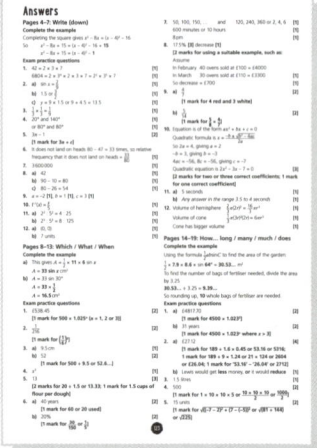

Mixed questions help to refine your exam skills with practice that recaps a variety of the command words.

An **index of topics** enables you to quickly find questions within the book from particular parts of the Edexcel GCSE specification.

Answers are given at the back of the book so that you can check and mark your own work.

Contents

Revise by command word!

Write (down)	4
Which / What / When	8
How… long / many / much / does	14
Work out / Find	20
Calculate	26
Change / Express	30
Simplify (fully)	32
Expand	36
Factorise (fully)	40
Solve / Make … the subject of the formula	44
Match (each graph) / Mark	48
Complete	52
Estimate	56
Draw / Sketch	60
Is … correct?	66
Use (a given method)	70
Translate / Reflect / Rotate / Enlarge	76
Describe	80
Construct	86
Give your answer	92
Give a reason	96
Explain / Justify	102
Prove that / Show (that)	106
Mixed Questions	112
Index of Topics	120
Answers	123

Write (down)

Worked example and more!

Write: You may need to do some working to answer the question.

Write down: You should be able to answer the question without written workings.

TOP TIP
You can quickly check the answers to these questions if you have time.

Example question

1 Algebra • Grade 4–6

The graph of $y = x^2 - 4x$ is shown.

a) Write down the coordinates of the turning point. **(1)**

b) Write down the roots of $x^2 - 4x = 0$ **(1)**

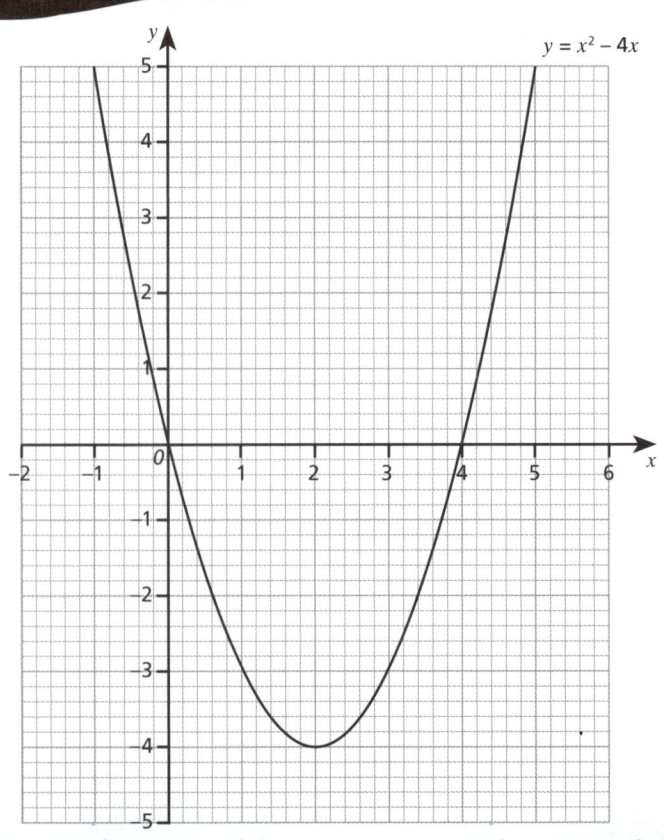

Complete the example

Algebra • Grade 7–9

Write $x^2 - 8x + 15$ in the form $(x - a)^2 + b$ (2)

Completing the square gives $x^2 - 8x = (x - 4)^2 - 16$

So $x^2 - 8x + 15 = (x - 4)^2 - 16 +$ _____

$x^2 - 8x + 15 = (x - 4)^2 -$ _____

Exam practice questions

1 Number • Grade 4–6

You are given that $162 = 2 \times 3^4$ and that $6804 = 162 \times 42$

Write 6804 as a product of prime factors in index form. (2)

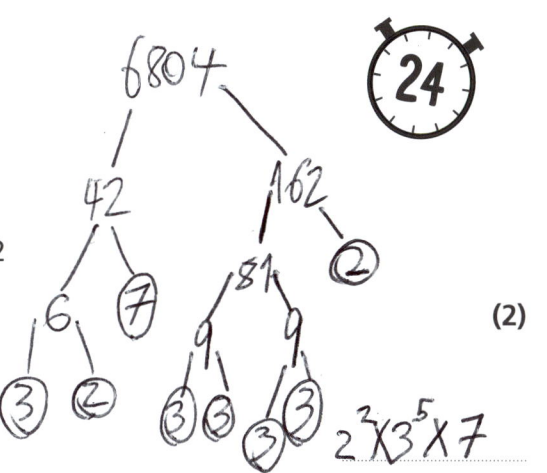

2³ × 3⁵ × 7

2 Geometry and Measures • Grade 4–6

Triangles A and B are similar.

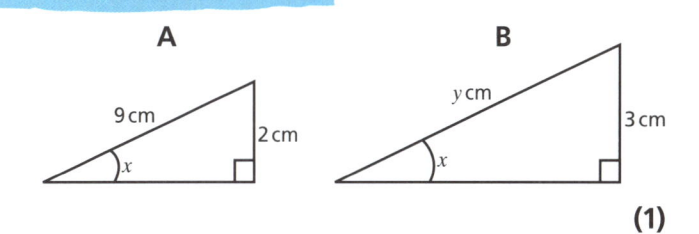

a) Write down the value of sin x. (1)

b) Write down the scale factor of enlargement from triangle A to triangle B. (1)

1.5

c) Use your answer to part b) or another method to write down the value of y. (1)

$y =$ *13.5*

3 Probability • Grade 4–6

This spinner is equally likely to land on each colour.
The spinner is spun twice.

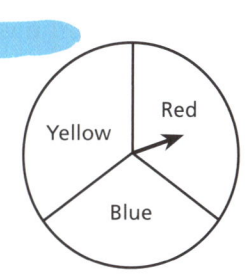

Write down the probability that it lands on yellow twice. (1)

1/9

4 Geometry and Measures • Grade 4–6

An isosceles triangle has one angle of 20°.

Write down the possible sizes of the other two angles. (2)

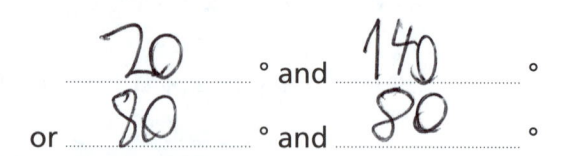

__20__° and __140__°

or __80__° and __80__°

5 Algebra • Grade 4–6

The first four terms of an arithmetic sequence are   2   5   8   11

Write down an expression for the nth term. (2)

$3n - 1$

6 Probability • Grade 4–6

A coin is thrown 80 times.
It lands on heads 47 times.

Write down the relative frequency that it does **not** land on heads. (1)

7 Number • Grade 4–6

Write 3.6×10^6 as an ordinary number. (1)

3600000

8 Statistics • Grade 7–9

Here is a box plot.

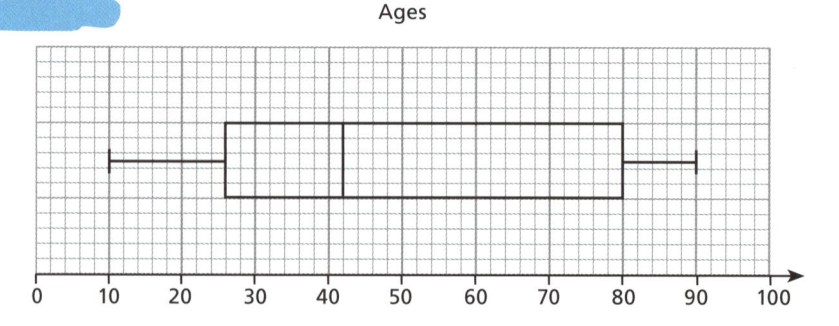

Ages

a) Write down the value of the median. (1)

42

b) Write down the value of the range. (1)

80

c) Write down the value of the interquartile range. (1)

54

9 Algebra • Grade 7–9

On the grid, the shaded triangle is described by these inequalities.

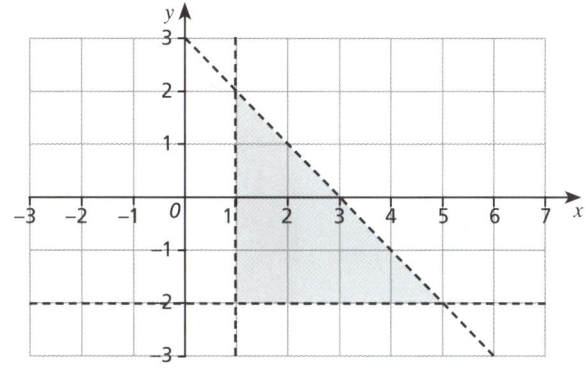

$y > a$
$x > b$
$y < -x + c$

Write down the values of a, b and c. (3)

$a = $ ...., $b = $ ...., $c = $ ....

10 Algebra • Grade 7–9

$f(x) = 5x$

Write down an expression for $f^{-1}(x)$ (1)

11 Ratio, Proportion and Rates of Change • Grade 7–9

Two cubes have sides in the ratio 2 : 5

a) Write down the ratio of their surface areas. (1)

b) Write down the ratio of their volumes. (1)

12 Geometry and Measures • Grade 7–9

The equation of a circle is $x^2 + y^2 = 49$

a) Write down the coordinates of the centre of the circle. (1)

(.................., ...)

b) Write down the radius of the circle. (1)

.... units

Total score: .... / 23

Which/What/When

Worked examples and more!

These are similar to 'work out' and 'write down' questions but asked in a more direct way.

TOP TIP
For some questions, but not all, working out will be required.

Example questions

1 **Number • Grade 4–6**

Which of these has the greatest value?

8.24×10^3 8.2×10^4 82 400 8.02×10^4 (1)

2 **Probability • Grade 7–9**

A game is played with three unbiased spinners.

Spinner X has eight sides   1, 2, 2, 3, 3, 3, 3, 4
Spinner Y has five sides   1, 2, 2, 3, 4
Spinner Z has four sides   1, 1, 1, 4

In the game, a player has two options.

Option A	Option B
Spin X and then spin Y	Spin Z two times

A player wins if the total of their two spins is exactly 5.

Which option has the better chance of winning?
You **must** show working to support your answer. (4)

Complete the example

Geometry and Measures • Grade 7–9

The diagram shows a triangle.

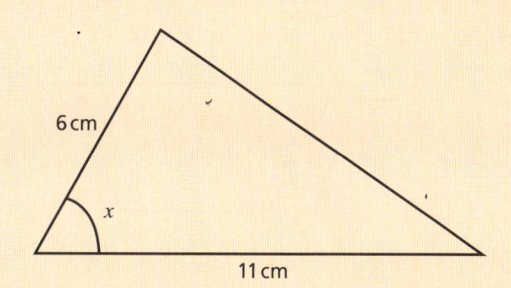

a) Which formula gives the area, A, in cm² for the triangle?

$A = 66 \sin x$ $A = 66 \cos x$ $A = 33 \sin x$ $A = 33 \cos x$ (1)

The formula for the area of a triangle with sides a and b is

Area = $\frac{1}{2} ab \sin C$, where C is the angle between a and b.

This gives $A = \frac{1}{2} \times$ _____ $\times$ _____ $\times \sin$ _____

$A =$ _____ cm²

b) $x = 30°$

What is the area? (1)

Substituting $x = 30°$ gives

$A =$ _____ $\sin 30°$

$A =$ _____ $\times$ ▢/▢

$A =$ _____ cm²

Exam practice questions

⏱ 35

1 Ratio, Proportion and Rates of Change • Grade 4–6

A savings account pays 2.5% compound interest per year.
£500 is invested in the account.

What is the total value after 3 years? (2)

£538.45

2. Probability • Grade 4–6

A fair, six-sided spinner is shown.
The spinner is spun three times and the letters are written down from left to right.

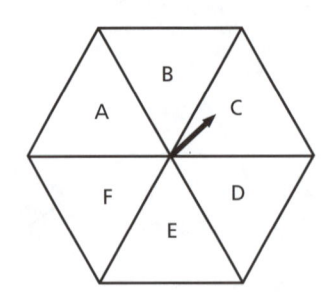

What is the probability that the word BAD is spelled out? (2)

$$\frac{1}{216}$$

3. Number • Grade 4–6

Pieces of tape are cut from a 5-metre roll.
Each piece of tape is 10 cm to the nearest centimetre.

a) What is the shortest possible length of a piece of tape? (1)

9.5 cm

b) What is the greatest number of pieces of tape that can be cut from the roll? (2)

502

4. Algebra • Grade 4–6

Which of these equations gives the smallest value for y when $x = -3$?

| $y = x^3$ | $y = 8x$ | $y = 2x^{-2}$ |

(1)

$y = -27$ $y = -24$ $y = 0.\dot{2}$

$y = x^3$

5 Ratio, Proportion and Rates of Change • Grade 4–6

A pizza dough recipe uses cups of flour and cups of yogurt in the ratio 3 : 2
Each pizza dough uses 1 cup of yogurt.

What is the maximum number of pizzas that can be made from 20 cups of flour and 20 cups of yogurt? (3)

6 Number / Statistics • Grade 4–6

The table shows the ages of 150 people at a party.

Age, A (years)	$10 \leq A < 20$	$20 \leq A < 40$	$40 \leq A < 60$	$60 \leq A < 90$
Frequency	23	65	32	30

a) What is the minimum possible age range of the people? (2)

$10 \leq A \leq 20$ years

b) What percentage of the people are 60 or over? (2)

20 %

7 Number • Grade 4–6

A green light and a red light flash together at 10 am.
The green light flashes every 50 minutes.
The red light flashes every 2 hours.

When will the two lights next flash together? (3)

Green 10 am   10:50am   11:40am   12:20pm   1pm
Red   10 am   12pm   2pm   4pm   6pm   8pm
       1:50pm 2:40pm   3:20pm   4pm
       10pm   12am

4pm

8 Ratio, Proportion and Rates of Change • Grade 7–9

A shop increased the price of its ovens by 10% on 1st March.
The number sold in March was $\frac{1}{4}$ less than in February.

By what percentage did the income from the sales of ovens change in March?
Remember to state whether it is an increase or decrease. (4)

9 Probability • Grade 7–9

A bag contains 5 red balls and 3 white balls.
A ball is chosen from the bag at random and **not** replaced.
Another ball is then chosen from the bag at random.

a) What is the probability that the second ball is red, given that the first one was red? (2)

b) What is the probability that **both** balls are red? (2)

10 Algebra • Grade 7–9

Richard is trying to solve a quadratic equation.
This is his correct substitution into the quadratic formula.

$$x = \frac{3 \pm \sqrt{9 + 56}}{4}$$

What is the quadratic equation he is trying to solve? (3)

11 Algebra • Grade 7–9

The graph shows the height of a drone for the first 10 seconds of a flight.

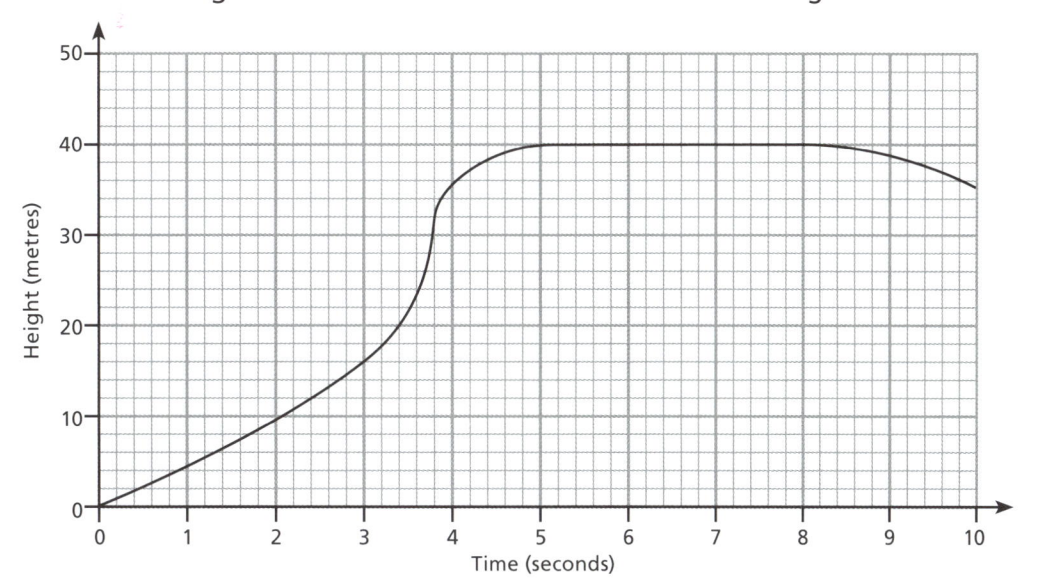

a) When does the drone first reach a height of 40 metres? (1)

.... seconds

b) When is the drone climbing at its fastest speed? (1)

.... seconds

12 Geometry and Measures • Grade 7–9

A cone and a hemisphere are shown.

Volume of a cone = $\frac{1}{3}\pi r^2 h$

Volume of a sphere = $\frac{4}{3}\pi r^3$

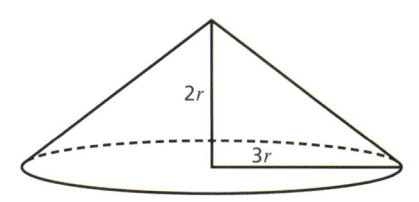

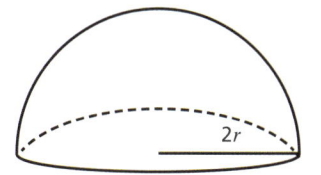

Cone: height $2r$, radius $3r$
Hemisphere: radius $2r$

Which shape has the bigger volume?
You **must** show working to support your answer. (3)

Total score: .... / 34

How... long/many/much/does

How long
How many
How much: **Give a counted, measured or calculated answer.**

How does this affect: **Make a comment or a comparison to state how the answer changes in a given situation.**

Worked examples and more!

TOP TIP
You may need to do more than one step to answer the question.

Example questions

1 Number • Grade 4–6

The value of a car is expected to fall by 10% each year.
The car is worth £16 000 when new.

How much would be the expected value of the car in 4 years? (3)

2 Algebra • Grade 7–9

The equation of a circle is $x^2 + y^2 = 64$

How long is the diameter of the circle? (1)

Complete the example

Geometry and Measures • Grade 7–9

The diagram shows a triangular garden.

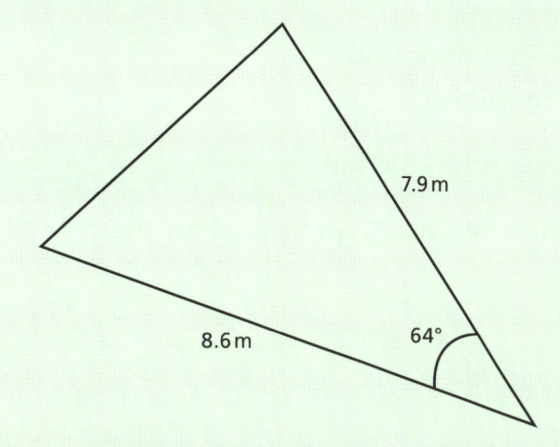

[Triangle with sides 7.9 m, 8.6 m and included angle 64°]

One bag of fertiliser covers 3.25 m² of garden.

How many bags of fertiliser are needed to cover the garden?

Using the formula $\frac{1}{2} ab \sin C$ to find the area of the garden

$\frac{1}{2}$ × _____ × _____ × sin _____ ° = _____ m²

To find the number of bags of fertiliser needed, divide the area by 3.25

_____ ÷ 3.25 = _____

So rounding up, _____ whole bags of fertiliser are needed.

Exam practice questions

1 Ratio, Proportion and Rates of Change • Grade 4–6

£4500 is invested at a compound interest rate of 2.3% per year.

a) How much is the investment worth after 3 years? (2)

£ 4817.90

b) How many years will it take for the initial investment to double in value? (2)

31 years

2 Ratio, Proportion and Rates of Change • Grade 4–6

Lewis drives his car for a job.
He claims 45p per mile from his employer.

1 mile = 1.6 km

The car travels 9 km per litre of petrol.
He pays £1.24 per litre for petrol.

a) On one journey Lewis drives 189 km.

   How much **more** does he claim than he pays for petrol on this journey? (4)

   £ ....

b) If the price of petrol increases, how does this affect your answer to part a)? (1)

   ....

3 Ratio, Proportion and Rates of Change • Grade 4–6

Liquid is poured into a container.
The graph shows the number of litres of liquid in the container.

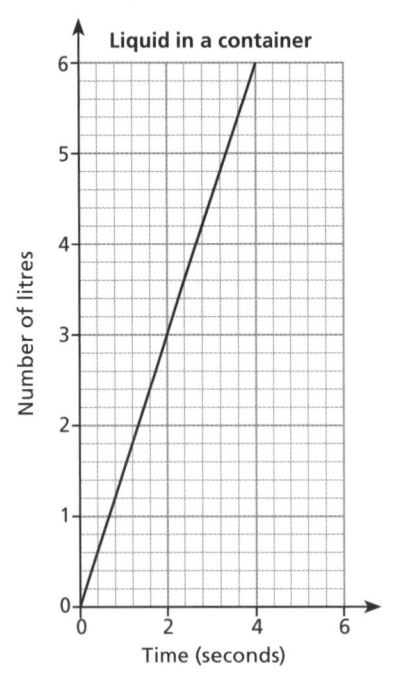

How much liquid is poured into the container each second? (1)

1.5 litres

4 Number • Grade 4–6

The code for a bike lock has four digits.
Each digit is a number from 0 to 9
Digits may be repeated.

0 1 2 3 4 5 6 7 8 9

The code begins with 2 and is an odd number.

2			

How many possible codes are there?

(2)

....

5 Geometry and Measures • Grade 4–6

The points A (–7, 7) and B (2, –5) are joined with a straight line.

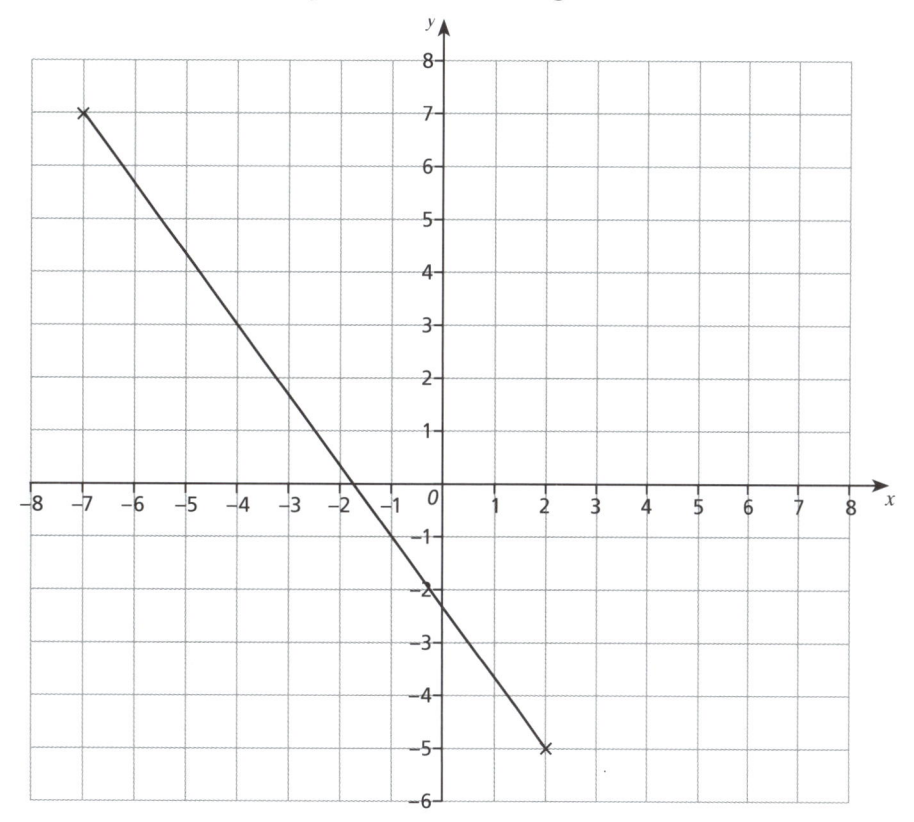

How long is the line? (2)

.... units

6 Geometry and Measures • Grade 7–9

Abi walks at a speed of 4.8 km/h from A to B, and then from B to C.
She then walks at the same speed from C to A.

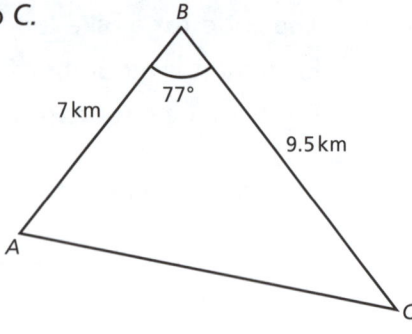

How long does it take Abi to walk from C to A?
Give your answer in hours and minutes.

(4)

.... hours .... minutes

7 Algebra • Grade 7–9

The graph shows the height above ground that a ball has been kicked.

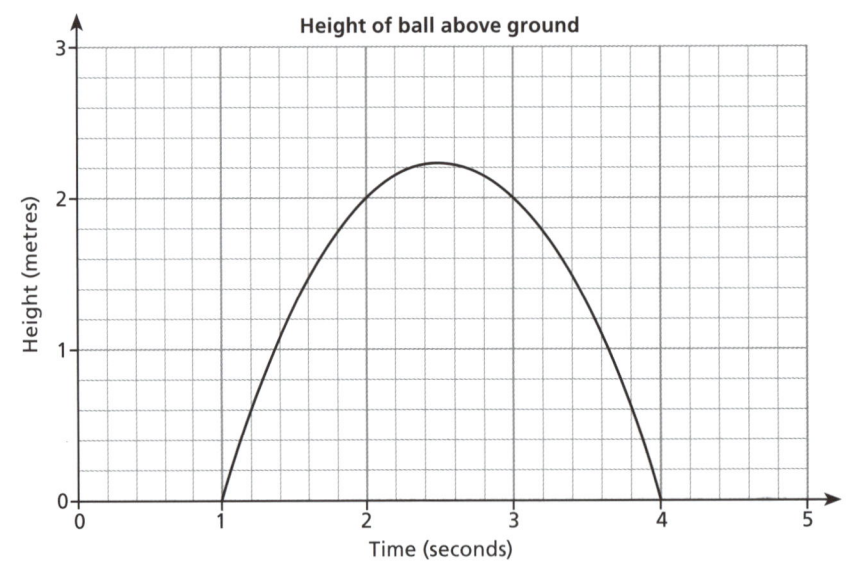

Height of ball above ground

a) For how long was the ball above the ground? (1)

.... seconds

b) How fast was the ball travelling after 2 seconds? (2)
    Show your working on the graph.

.... m/s

8 Geometry and Measures • Grade 7–9

Metal cuboids measure 30 cm by 30 cm by 7 cm.
A box contains 15 metal cuboids.
A machine is making spheres from the metal cuboids.

Volume of a sphere = $\frac{4}{3}\pi r^3$

How many spheres of radius 5 cm can the machine make from **one box** of cuboids? (6)

.... spheres

9 Statistics • Grade 7–9

A bus company records the number of minutes, t, some buses were late one week.
The histogram shows the results.

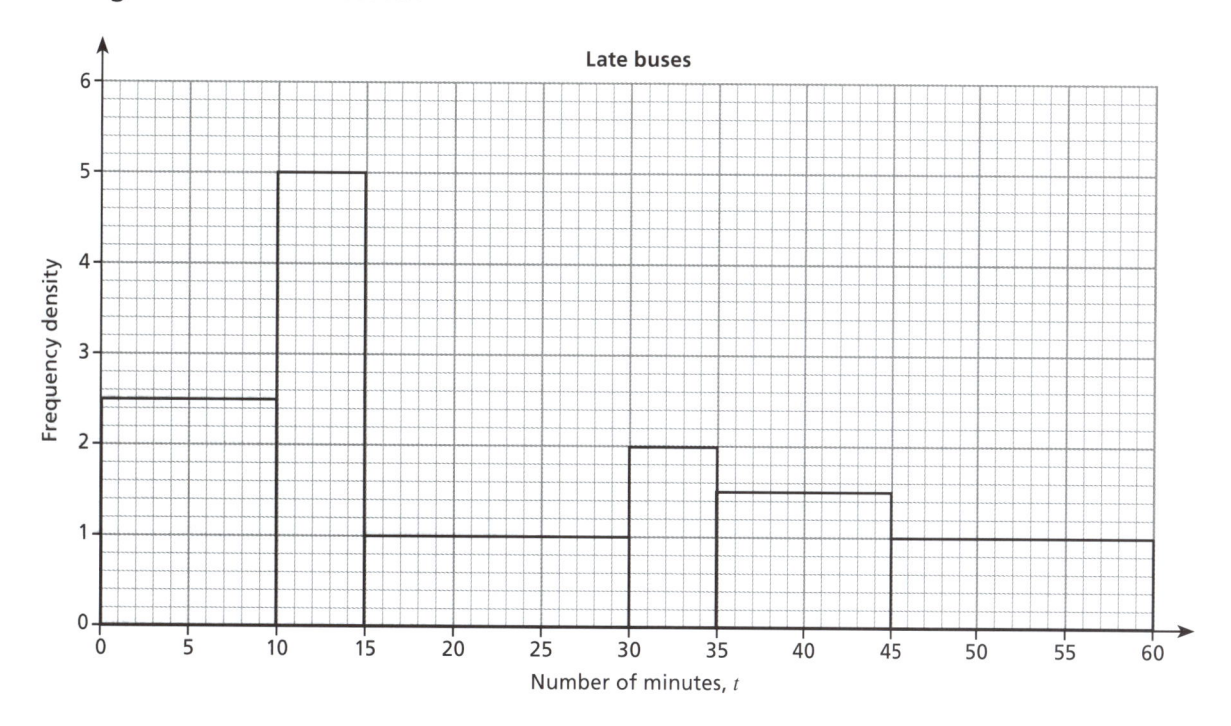

Estimate how many buses were more than 20 minutes late. (3)

Total score: .... / 30

Work out/ Find

Some working will usually be needed to get to the final answer of a given problem.

Worked examples and more!

TOP TIP You are likely to need to do one or more calculations.

Example questions

1 Ratio, Proportion and Rates of Change • Grade 4–6

In a sale, the price of a coat has been reduced by 15%
The sale price of the coat is £119

Find the price of the coat before the sale. (2)

2 Algebra • Grade 7–9

A cylinder has a radius of r.
An approximate value of r can be found using the iterative formula

$$r_{n+1} = \frac{7}{r_n^3} + 3$$

The starting value is $r_1 = 1$

a) Work out the values r_2 and r_3 (2)

b) Continue the iteration to work out the radius to 1 decimal place. (1)

Complete the example

Number • Grade 7–9

$a = \dfrac{b^2}{c}$

$b = 5.6$ to 1 decimal place
$c = 4.03$ to 2 decimal places

Work out the upper bound for the value for a.
Give your answer to 3 decimal places. (3)

For a to be as big as possible, we need the biggest value for the numerator (b^2) and the smallest value for the denominator (c).

So we use the upper bound for b and the lower bound for _____.

The upper bound for __b__ = __5.65__

The lower bound for __c__ = __4.025__

This gives the upper bound for $a = \dfrac{5.65^2}{4.025} = 7.931055901$

$a = $ __7.931__ to 3 d.p.

Exam practice questions

1 Number • Grade 4–6

You are given that

$84 = 2 \times 2 \times 3 \times 7$ $45 = 3 \times 3 \times 5$ $24 = 2 \times 2 \times 2 \times 3$

Find the lowest common multiple (LCM) of 84 and 45 and 24 (3)

9070

2 Algebra • Grade 4–6

Here is an identity.

$$a(4x - 3) \equiv bx + 15$$

Work out the values of a and b. (3)

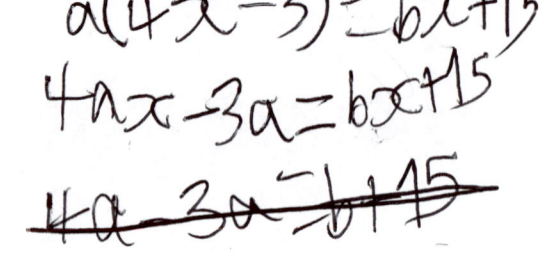

$a(4x-3) = bx+15$
$4ax - 3a = bx + 15$
~~$4a - 3a = b + 15$~~

$a = $ ....

$b = $ ....

3 Probability • Grade 4–6

Dylan travels to school by bus every day.
The probability the bus will be late each day is 0.08

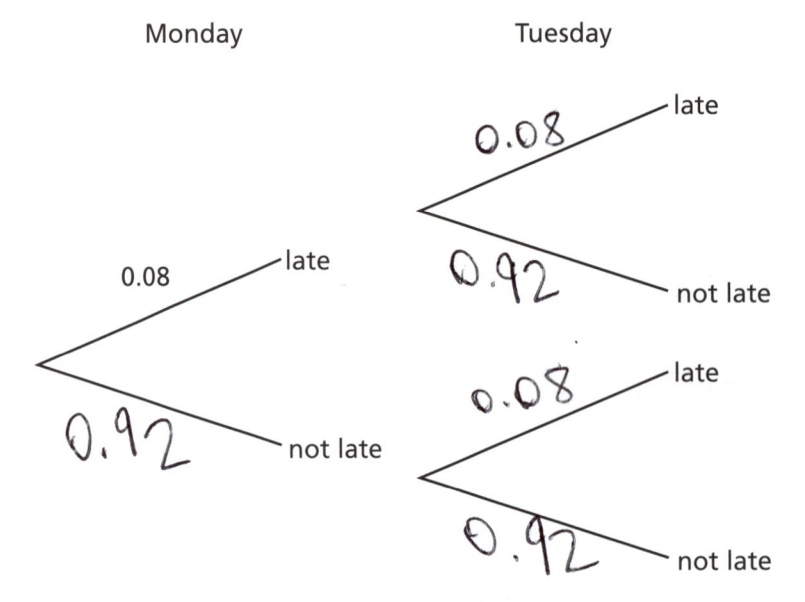

Monday / Tuesday tree diagram:
- Monday late: 0.08
  - Tuesday late: 0.08
  - Tuesday not late: 0.92
- Monday not late: 0.92
  - Tuesday late: 0.08
  - Tuesday not late: 0.92

Complete the tree diagram and work out the probability that the bus will be late on at least one of the two days. (4)

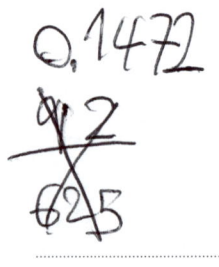

~~0.08~~

0.1472

~~2~~
~~625~~

4 Ratio, Proportion and Rates of Change • Grade 4–6

There are blue counters, green counters and red counters in a jar.
The ratio of the number of blue to green to red counters is   6 : 11 : 3

Work out the percentage of green counters in the jar. (2)

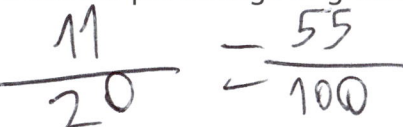

$$\frac{11}{20} = \frac{55}{100}$$

55 %

5 Geometry and Measures • Grade 4–6

XY and YZ are two sides of a regular 10-sided polygon.
XZ is a diagonal of the polygon.

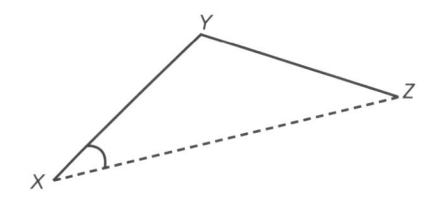

Find the size of angle YXZ. (3)

.... °

6 Geometry and Measures • Grade 7–9

The diagram shows two similar pieces of glass.

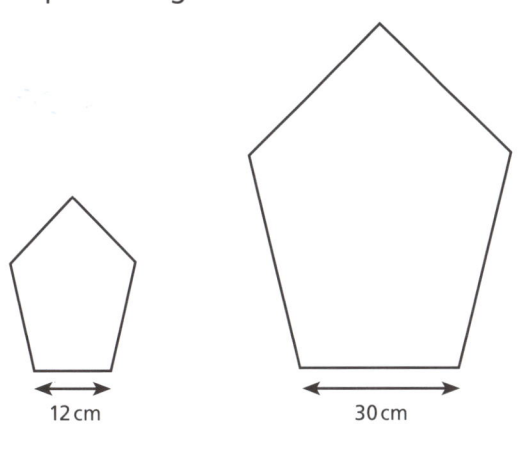

12 cm   30 cm

The area of the large piece is 1500 cm²

Work out the area of the small piece. (4)

.... cm²

7 Geometry and Measures • Grade 7–9

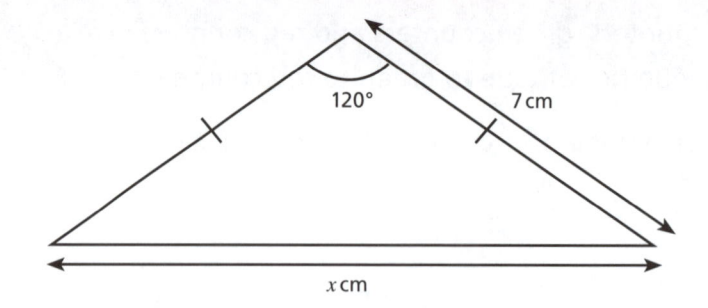

Given that sin 120° = sin 60°

Work out the value of x.

Give your answer in the form $a\sqrt{b}$ where a and b are integers. **(3)**

8 Algebra • Grade 7–9

Here are the first five terms of a quadratic sequence.

4, 9, 18, 31, 48

Find an expression, in terms of n, for the nth term of the sequence. **(3)**

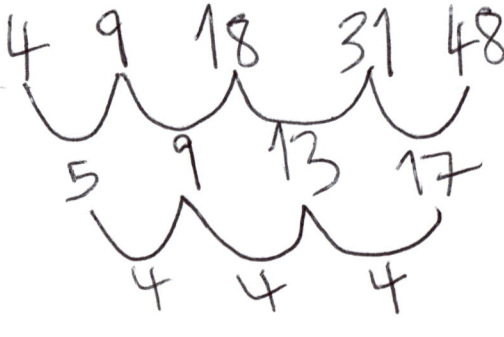

9 Algebra • Grade 7–9

You are given that $f(x) = x^2 - 15$ and $g(x) = x - 4$

Find an expression for $fg(x)$ **(2)**

10 Algebra • Grade 7–9

$3x^2 + ax + 4 \equiv (3x + b)(x + c)$

Work out all possible values of a when b and c are integers. (3)

11 Algebra • Grade 7–9

The graph of $y = f(x)$ is shown.

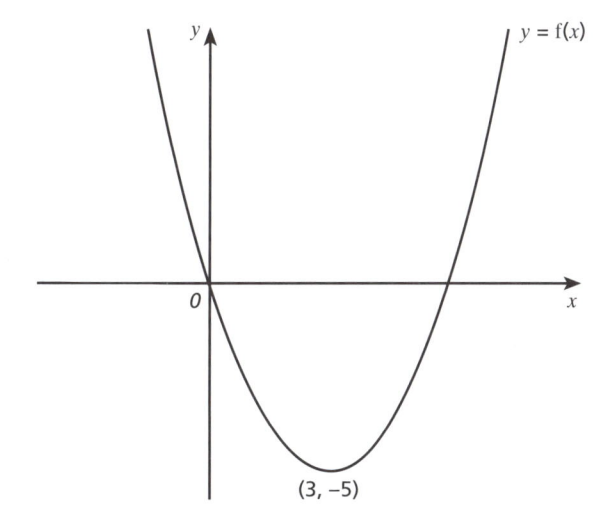

(3, –5)

The coordinates of the turning point of the curve are (3, –5).

Find the coordinates of the turning point of the curve with equation $y = f(x + 3)$ (1)

(........., ...)

Calculate

Worked examples and more!

[QR code]

These are similar to 'work out' questions but may be more difficult and you may need to use your calculator.

TOP TIP
For most questions, working out will be required.

Example questions

1 Geometry and Measures • Grade 4–6

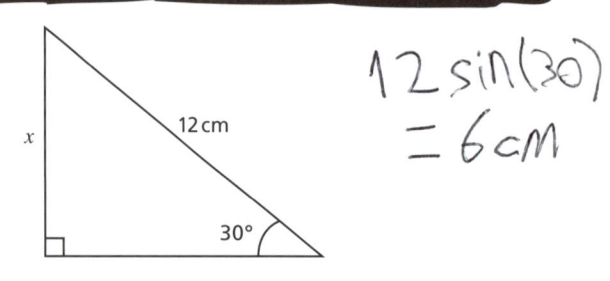

Using trigonometry, calculate the length x. (3)

$12 \sin(30)$
$= 6 cm$

2 Geometry and Measures • Grade 7–9

The area of triangle *XYZ* is 90 cm²

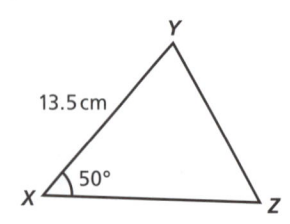

Calculate the length of side *XZ*.
Give your answer to 3 significant figures. (2)

Complete the example

Number / Algebra / Geometry and Measures • Grade 7–9

Calculate the area of the trapezium.
Give your answer in the form $(a\sqrt{3} + b)$ cm², where a and b are integers. (3)

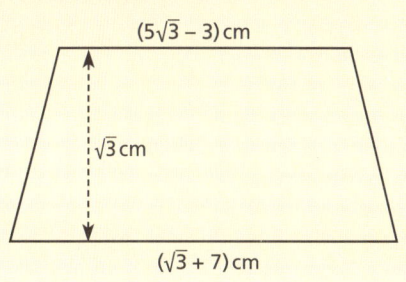

Trapezium with parallel sides $(5\sqrt{3} - 3)$ cm (top) and $(\sqrt{3} + 7)$ cm (bottom), and height $\sqrt{3}$ cm.

The formula for the area of a trapezium is $\quad \frac{1}{2}(a+b)h$

Substituting in the lengths from the diagram gives $\quad \frac{1}{2}(\ldots\ldots) \times \ldots\ldots$

Simplifying the bracket gives $\quad \frac{1}{2}(\ldots\ldots) \times \ldots\ldots$

Multiplying the bracket by $\frac{1}{2}$ gives $\quad (\ldots\ldots) \times \ldots\ldots$

The area of the trapezium is $\quad \ldots\ldots$ cm²

Exam practice questions

⏱ 28

1 Ratio, Proportion and Rates of Change • Grade 4–6

Gaby and Talin share £240 in the ratio $\quad$ 3.8 : 1

Calculate how much more Gaby gets than Talin. (3)

$3.8 : 1 = 4.8$
$19 : 5 = 24$
$190 : 50 = 240$

$190 - 50$

£ 140

2 Algebra • Grade 4–6

You are given that $\quad \frac{b}{3c} = 2 \quad$ and $\quad \frac{2a}{b} = c^2$

Calculate the value of a when $c = 5$ (3)

$\frac{b}{3c} = 2 \quad \frac{b}{15} = 2 \quad b = 30$

$\frac{2a}{30} = 25 \quad 2a = 750$
$a = 375$

$a = 375$

3 Geometry and Measures • Grade 4–6

A wooden hammer is made from a cuboid and a cylinder, radius r, as shown.

The total volume is 1200 cm³

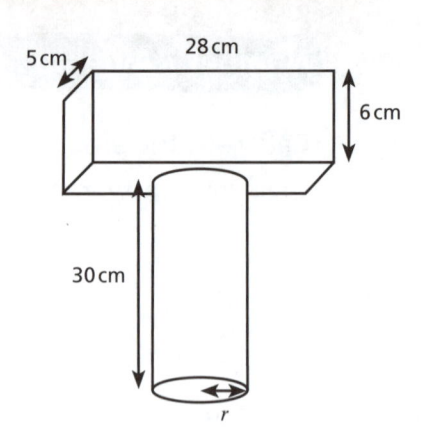

(Diagram: cuboid 28 cm × 5 cm × 6 cm with cylinder of height 30 cm and radius r below)

Calculate the value of r.
Give your answer to 3 significant figures. (5)

$r = $ .... cm

4 Number • Grade 4–6

The distance from Earth to Pluto is approximately 5.1×10^{12} metres.
The speed of light is 3×10^8 metres per second.

Calculate the time it will take in hours for light to travel from Earth to Pluto.
Give your answer to 3 significant figures. (3)

.... hours

5 Geometry and Measures • Grade 4–6

In this diagram, MP and QS are parallel.

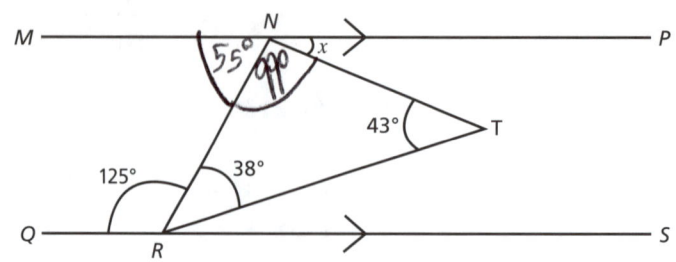

(Diagram showing angles: 55°, x, 43°, 125°, 38° at points M, N, P, Q, R, S, T)

Calculate the size of angle x. (3)

$x = $ **26** °

6 Algebra • Grade 7–9

a is inversely proportional to the cube of b.
When $a = 9.6$, $b = 2.5$

Calculate the value of b when $a = 1.2$ (3)

$b =$ ....

7 Probability • Grade 7–9

A bag contains 3 blue balls and y green balls.
Tom takes a ball from the bag at random, records its colour and puts it back.
He then takes another ball from the bag at random.
The probability that both balls are blue is $\frac{9}{25}$

Calculate the number of balls that were in the bag to begin with. (2)

....

8 Geometry and Measures • Grade 7–9

ABCDE is a regular pentagon.

The area of triangle ABE is 25 cm²

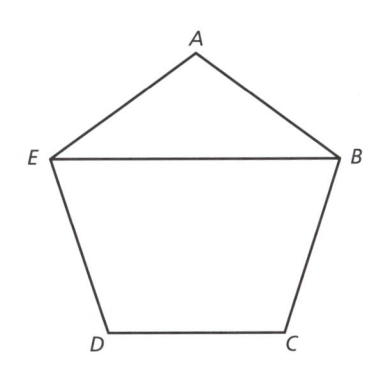

Calculate the length of EB.
Give your answer correct to 3 significant figures.
You **must** show your working. (5)

$EB =$ .... cm

Total score: .... / 27

Change/Express

Change: Convert a value from one numerical form to another, or a measure from one unit to another. You may need to use a calculation or read from a conversion graph.

Express: Write a number in another form, e.g. a fraction or ratio in its simplest form.

Worked examples and more!

TOP TIP
Make sure you can convert between metric units of length, area, volume (capacity) and mass, as well as between different units of time.

Example questions

1 Number • Grade 4–6

Change 270 kilometres per hour to metres per second. (3)

2 Algebra • Grade 7–9

Change the quadratic expression $2x^2 - 10x + 13$ into the form $a(x + b)^2 + c$ (3)

Complete the example

Number • Grade 7–9

Express $2\sqrt{125}$ in the form $a\sqrt{5}$ where a is a positive integer. (2)

$2\sqrt{125} = 2\sqrt{25 \times \text{\_\_\_\_}} \qquad = 2\sqrt{25} \times \sqrt{\text{\_\_\_\_}}$

$\qquad = 2 \times \text{\_\_\_\_} \sqrt{\text{\_\_\_\_}} \qquad = \text{\_\_\_\_} \sqrt{5}$

Exam practice questions

⏱ 10

1 Number • Grade 4–6

Change 12 m² to cm² (2)

~~1200~~ cm²

2 Number • Grade 4–6

Express $\sqrt{\dfrac{10^6 \times 10^4}{10^8}}$ as a power of 10 (2)

3 Ratio, Proportion and Rates of Change • Grade 4–6

You are given that
1 pound (lb) = 454 grams (g) and 1 square inch (inch²) = 6.45 square centimetres (cm²)

The foot of a young elephant exerts a pressure of 5.5 pounds per square inch (lb/inch²) on the ground.

Change 5.5 pounds per square inch to grams per square centimetre (g/cm²).
Give your answer to 1 decimal place. (3)

____ g/cm²

4 Number • Grade 7–9

Change the recurring decimal $0.4\dot{2}\dot{7}$ to a fraction in its simplest form. (3)

Total score: ____ / 10

Simplify (fully)

Simplify: Collect terms or cancel a fraction.

Simplify fully: Collect terms or cancel a fraction to its lowest terms.

Worked examples and more!

TOP TIP
The word 'fully' suggests more than one step is necessary.

Example questions

1 Algebra • Grade 4–6

Simplify fully $\quad \dfrac{4}{x} + \dfrac{5}{2x}$ (2)

2 Number • Grade 7–9

Simplify $\quad \sqrt{3x^2} \times \sqrt{75x^3}$

Write your answer in the form $ax^{\frac{b}{c}}$ where a, b and c are integers. (3)

Complete the example

Algebra • Grade 7–9

Simplify fully $\dfrac{x+2}{5} - \dfrac{x-3}{4}$ (3)

$= \dfrac{\rule{0.5cm}{0.15mm}(x+2)}{\rule{0.5cm}{0.15mm}} - \dfrac{\rule{0.5cm}{0.15mm}(x-3)}{\rule{0.5cm}{0.15mm}}$

$= \dfrac{\rule{0.5cm}{0.15mm} + 8}{20} - \dfrac{\rule{0.5cm}{0.15mm} - \rule{0.5cm}{0.15mm}}{20}$

$= \dfrac{\rule{0.5cm}{0.15mm} + \rule{0.5cm}{0.15mm} - \rule{0.5cm}{0.15mm} + \rule{0.5cm}{0.15mm}}{20}$

$= \dfrac{\rule{0.5cm}{0.15mm} + \rule{0.5cm}{0.15mm}}{20}$

Exam practice questions

⏲ 28

1. Algebra / Statistics • Grade 4–6

The upper quartile of a set of data is $7x + 2$
The lower quartile of the same set of data is $3x - 5$

Work out an expression for the interquartile range of the set of data.
Simplify your answer. (2)

$(7x+2) - (3x-5)$
$7x - 2 - 3x + 5$
$4x$

$4x + 3$

2. Algebra • Grade 4–6

a) Simplify $(2x^{-2})^5$ (1)

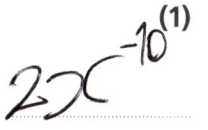

$2x^{-10}$

b) Simplify $\dfrac{27x^6}{9x^{-1}}$ (1)

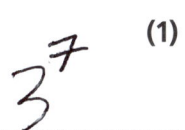

3^7

c) Simplify $\dfrac{4(x+y)^5}{2(x+y)^8}$ (1)

d) Simplify $\dfrac{x^2 y^7}{x^3 y}$ (1)

$x^{-1} y^6$

e) Simplify $\left(\dfrac{1}{x^3}\right)^0$ (1)

3 Algebra • Grade 4–6

Simplify fully $\dfrac{9f - 6g}{6f^2 - 4fg}$ (3)

4 Geometry and Measures • Grade 4–6

The diagram shows a trapezium.

The lengths of the two parallel sides are a cm and $7a$ cm.
The height of the trapezium is $5a$ cm.

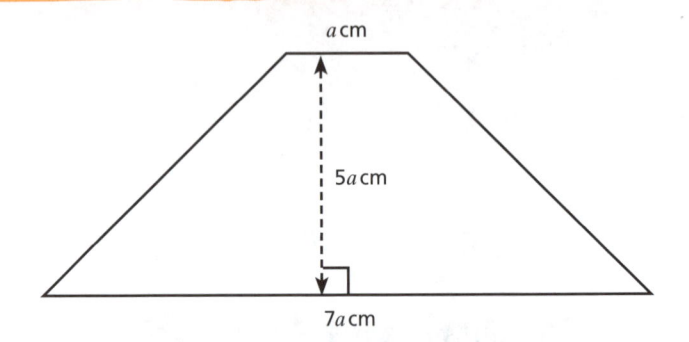

Work out an expression for the area of the trapezium.
Simplify your answer. (2)

.... cm²

5 Geometry and Measures • Grade 4–6

The diagram shows a cylinder.

The diameter of the cylinder is $400a$ centimetres.
The height of the cylinder is $3a$ metres.

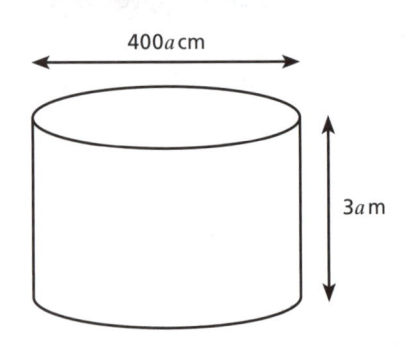

Work out an expression for the total surface area of the cylinder in m²
Simplify your answer. (3)

.... m²

6 Algebra • Grade 7–9

Simplify fully $\dfrac{4x^2 - 9}{2x^2 - x - 3}$ (3)

7 Algebra • Grade 7–9

Simplify $\left[(x+4) \div \dfrac{x^2 + x - 12}{x - 2}\right] + 3$

Give your answer in the form $\dfrac{ax - b}{x - c}$ where a, b and c are integers. (4)

8 Number • Grade 7–9

Simplify fully $\dfrac{(5 + 3\sqrt{2})(5 - 3\sqrt{2})}{7}$

You **must** show all your working. (2)

9 Number / Geometry and Measures • Grade 7–9

Simplify $\cos 45° + 2 \tan 45° - \sin 30°$

Give your answer in the form $\dfrac{a + \sqrt{b}}{c}$ where a, b and c are integers. (3)

$\dfrac{\sqrt{2}}{2} + \dfrac{2}{1} - \dfrac{1}{2}$

$\dfrac{\sqrt{2} + 4 - 1}{2}$ $\dfrac{3 + \sqrt{2}}{2}$ $\dfrac{3 + \sqrt{2}}{2}$

Total score: / 27

Expand

Remove the brackets. In some questions, working out will be required and should be shown. You will usually need to simplify answers.

Worked examples and more!

TOP TIP
Collect like terms where possible.

Example questions

1 Algebra • Grade 4–6

Expand and simplify $(2a + 3)^2$ (3)

2 Algebra • Grade 7–9

Expand and simplify $(5 + \sqrt{3})^2 - (5 - \sqrt{3})^2$ (3)

Complete the example

Number • Grade 7–9

Expand and simplify $(7 - \sqrt{3})(5 + 2\sqrt{3})$

Give your answer in the form $a + b\sqrt{3}$, where a and b are integers. (2)

Multiplying each term in the first bracket by each term in the second bracket gives

$7 \times 5 =$ _____ $7 \times 2\sqrt{3} =$ _____

and

$-\sqrt{3} \times$ _____ $=$ _____ $-\sqrt{3} \times$ _____ $=$ _____

Adding all the terms gives   _____ + _____ − _____ − _____

The final answer is   _____ + _____ $\sqrt{3}$

Exam practice questions

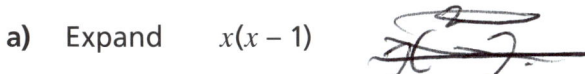

1 Algebra • Grade 4–6

a) Expand $x(x - 1)$ (1)

$x^2 - x$

b) Expand and simplify $x - (x + 1)$ (1)

2 Algebra • Grade 4–6

a) Expand $5x(x^2 + 6)$ (2)

b) Expand $2y^2(y^2 + 7y + 3)$ (2)

3 Algebra • Grade 4–6

a) Expand and simplify $(y + 5)(y - 4)$ (2)

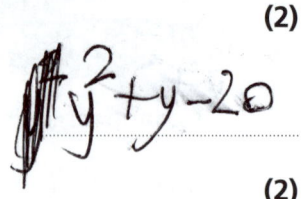

$y^2 - 4y + 5y - 20$

$y^2 + y - 20$

b) Expand and simplify $(2x - 7)(3x + 1)$ (2)

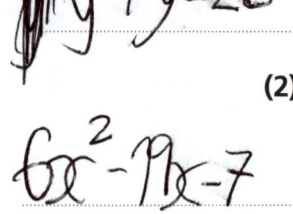

$6x^2 + 2x - 21x - 7$

$6x^2 - 19x - 7$

c) Expand and simplify $(a + b)(a - b)$ (2)

$a^2 - ab$

4 Algebra • Grade 4–6

Expand $(2x + 5)(3x - 4) - x(6x + 7)$ to show that it simplifies to an integer.   (3)

5 Algebra • Grade 7–9

Expand and simplify $(x - 1)(x + 2)(x + 3)$ (3)

6 Algebra • Grade 7–9

Expand and simplify $(2x + 3)(x - 2)^2$ (3)

7 Algebra • Grade 7–9

Expand and simplify $(2y^2 - 3)(3y + 7) - 5y(y^2 - 4)$ (4)

8 Number • Grade 7–9

a) Expand and simplify $(4 + \sqrt{5})^2$ (2)

b) Expand and simplify $(2\sqrt{3} - 3)^2$ (2)

9 Algebra / Geometry and Measures • Grade 7–9

The diagram shows a cuboid.

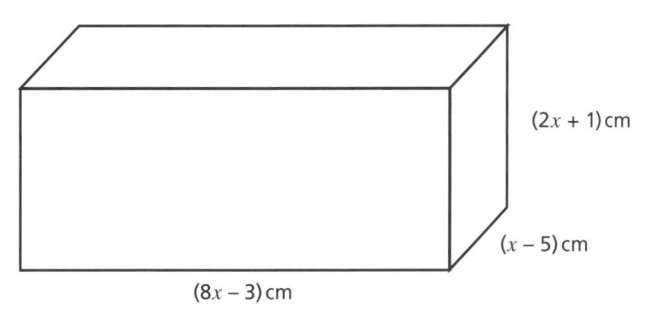

$(2x + 1)$ cm
$(x - 5)$ cm
$(8x - 3)$ cm

Expand the expressions for the length, width and height of the cuboid to obtain the volume of the cuboid in the form $ax^3 + bx^2 + cx + d$ (3)

10 Number • Grade 7–9

Expand and simplify fully (4)

$$\sqrt{\tfrac{1}{2} + 1} \times \sqrt{\tfrac{1}{3} + 1} \times \sqrt{\tfrac{1}{4} + 1} \times \sqrt{\tfrac{1}{5} + 1} \times \sqrt{\tfrac{1}{6} + 1} \times \sqrt{\tfrac{1}{7} + 1}$$

Total score: / 36

Factorise (fully)

Take out any common factors or convert a quadratic expression into two linear factors. This should always be done fully, even if that word is not in the question.

Worked examples and more!

TOP TIP
The word 'fully' is a hint that more than one factor can be taken out.

Example questions

1 Algebra • Grade 4–6

Factorise fully $54x^2yz - 36x^3y^3z^2$ (2)

2 Algebra • Grade 7–9

Factorise fully $\frac{4}{9}x^2 - 1$ (2)

Complete the example

Algebra • Grade 7–9

Factorise $3x^2 - 13x - 10$ (2)

This is a quadratic expression in the form $ax^2 + bx + c$ and it will factorise into two linear brackets. The method used here to factorise an expression where $a > 1$ is to compare ac and b. You may know a different method.

$ac =$ _____ $b =$ _____

Two numbers that multiply to equal ac (_____) and add to equal b (_____) are _____ and _____

This gives you the coefficients of the x term in the expansion.

Rewriting the quadratic expression, replacing $-13x$ with $-15x + 2x$

$3x^2 -$ _____ $x +$ _____ $x - 10$

Factorising the first two terms and then the second two terms separately

_____ $(x -$ _____$) +$ _____ $(x -$ _____$)$

The final factorised answer is therefore $($_____$)($_____$)$

Check your answer by multiplying out the brackets.

Exam practice questions

⏱ 28

1 Algebra • Grade 4–6

a) Factorise $x^2 + 6x$ (1)

$x(x+6)$

b) Factorise fully $15a^3b - 20ab^2$ (2)

$5ab(3a^2 - 4b)$

c) Factorise fully $22c^4d^5 - 11c^5d^7 + 77cd^3$ (2)

2 Algebra • Grade 4–6

a) Factorise $a^2 + 10a + 21$ (2)

b) Factorise $b^2 + 3b - 10$ (2)

c) Factorise $c^2 - 13c + 36$ (2)

3 Algebra • Grade 4–6

a) Factorise $a^2 - 25$ (1)

b) Factorise $9b^2 - 1$ (1)

c) Factorise fully $8c^2 - 98$ (2)

d) Factorise fully $4d^5 - 9d$ (2)

4 Algebra • Grade 7–9

a) Factorise $\quad 3h^2 - 11h - 4$ (2)

b) Factorise $\quad 6g^2 - 13g + 6$ (2)

5 Algebra • Grade 7–9

Factorise $\quad \frac{1}{4}x^2 + \frac{3}{2}x + 2$ (2)

6 Algebra • Grade 7–9

Factorise $\quad x^2 + 2\sqrt{2}x + 2$ (2)

7 Algebra • Grade 7–9

Factorise $\quad 5x^2 - 13xy + 6y^2$ (2)

Total score: / 27

Solve/Make ... the subject of the formula

Solve: Work out the value or values that satisfy a given equation or inequality.

Make ... the subject of the formula: Rearrange the given formula with a different subject as specified in the question.

Worked examples and more!

TOP TIP
Take a step-by-step approach to solving equations and rearranging formulae.

Example questions

1 Algebra • Grade 4–6

Solve $7x - 19 \leqslant 4(x - 1)$ (3)

2 Algebra • Grade 7–9

Make a the subject of the formula

$$\frac{a^2 - 7}{a^2 + 4} = b$$ (4)

Complete the example

Algebra • Grade 7–9

Make x the subject of the formula $\quad y = \dfrac{3x+8}{x-2}$ (4)

Multiplying both sides by $(x-2)$ gives ____(____ − ____) = ____ + ____

Expanding the brackets ____ − ____ = ____ + ____

Rearranging to move the x terms to the left-hand side and the numbers to the right-hand side ____ − ____ = ____ + ____

Factorising $x($____$) = $ ____ $+ 2y$

Dividing both sides by the bracket $x = $ ____

Exam practice questions

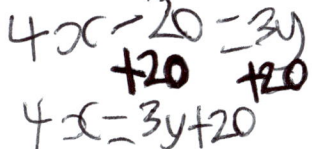

1 Algebra • Grade 4–6

Make x the subject of the formula $\quad 4(x-5) = 3y$ (2)

$4x - 20 = 3y$
$\quad +20 \quad +20$
$4x = 3y + 20$

$x = \dfrac{3y+20}{4}$

2 Algebra • Grade 4–6

Solve $\quad x^2 + 14x - 32 = 0$ (3)

$P = -32$
$S = 14$

$(x+16)(x-2)$

$x = -16$ or $x = 2$

3 Algebra • Grade 4–6

Solve $\quad 2x - y = 3$
$\quad\quad\quad x - 3y = \dfrac{13}{2}$ (4)

$2x - y = 3$
$2x - 6y = 13$
$-5y = 10$

$x = $ ____

$y = $ ____

4 Algebra • Grade 4–6

Solve $60.8 - 5x = 14x$ (2)

$+5x \quad +5x$

$60.8 = 19x$

$3.2 = x$

$x = 3.2$

5 Algebra • Grade 4–6

Solve $6x + 11 > x - 3$ (2)

$6x + 11 > x - 3$
$\quad +3 \quad\quad +3$
$6x + 14 > x$
$\quad -14 \quad -14$
$6x > x - 14$
$-x \quad -x$
$5x > -14$

6 Algebra • Grade 7–9

Solve $2x^2 - 8x + 3 = 0$ (3)

Give your solutions to 2 decimal places.

$x = $ _____ or $x = $ _____

7 Algebra • Grade 7–9

Make x the subject of the formula $y = \dfrac{x + 1}{3 - 2x}$ (4)

8 Algebra • Grade 7–9

Solve the inequality $x^2 > 6x$ (2)

9 Algebra • Grade 7–9

Solve the quadratic equation by completing the square.

$$x^2 - 6x - 27 = 0$$

You **must** show your working. (3)

$x =$ .... or $x =$ ....

10 Algebra • Grade 7–9

Solve $\dfrac{2}{2x-3} + \dfrac{3}{x+1} = 1$ (4)

$x =$ .... or $x =$ ....

Total score: .... / 29

Match (each graph)/Mark

Worked example and more!

Match (each graph): Decide which graph best fits with each equation in the table and write the correct answer for each one.

Mark: Identify the correct position of a point on a graph or diagram.

> **TOP TIP**
> Read the question carefully to make sure you answer as asked.

Example question

1 Geometry and Measures • Grade 4–6

The diagram shows the position of two boats, A and B.

Boat C is on a bearing of 045° from boat A.
Boat C is on a bearing of 320° from boat B.

On the diagram, accurately show the position of boat C.
Mark the position of boat C with a cross (X) and label it C. (3)

Complete the example

Algebra • Grade 7–9

Here are four graphs, A, B, C and D.

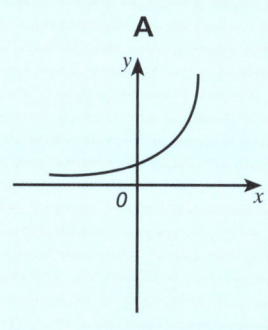

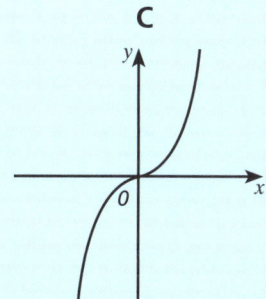

A

B

C

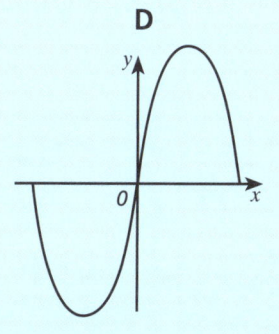

D

Here are five equations.

$y = \dfrac{1}{x}$ $y = -x^2 - 2$ $y = \sin x$ $y = 2^x$ $y = x^3$

Match each graph to the correct equation. (3)

Remember that:
- quadratic graphs can be written in the form $y = ax^2 + bx + c$
- cubic graphs can be written in the form $y = ax^3$
- exponential graphs can be written in the form $y = a^x$
- trigonometric graphs can be written in the form $y = \sin x$ or $y = \cos x$ or $y = \tan x$

A is $y = $ ....

B is $y = $ ....

C is $y = $ ....

D is $y = $ ....

Exam practice questions

1. Algebra • Grade 4–6

a) Mark the turning point of this quadratic function with a cross (✗).

(1)

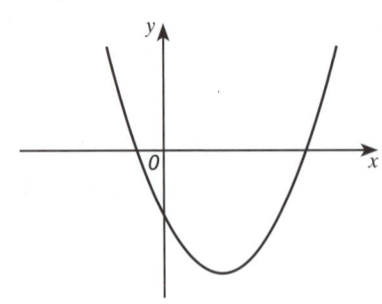

b) Mark the roots of this quadratic function with crosses (✗).

(1)

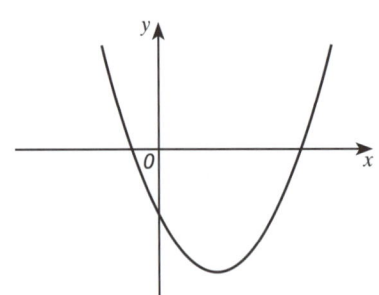

2. Geometry and Measures • Grade 4–6

The diagram shows the position of two towns.

Town F is on a bearing of 115° from town D and on a bearing of 230° from town E.

On the diagram, accurately show the position of town F.
Mark the position of town F with a cross (✗) and label it F.

(3)

3 Algebra • Grade 7–9

Here are graphs A, B, C and D.

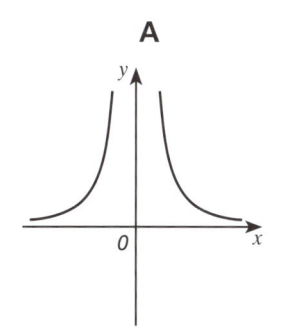

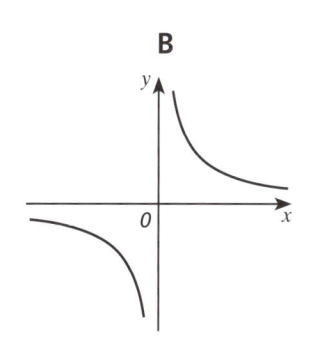

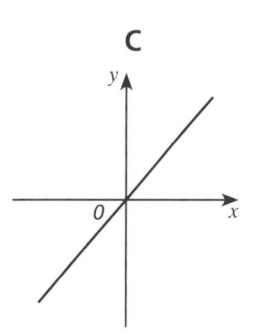

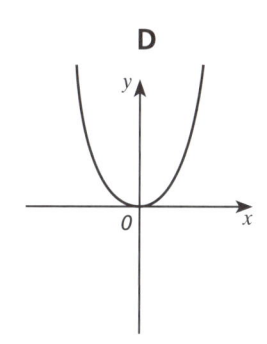

A B C D

Match each graph with a statement in the table below.

Proportionality relationship	Graph
y is directly proportional to x	
y is inversely proportional to x	
y is proportional to the square of x	
y is inversely proportional to the square of x	

(2)

4 Algebra • Grade 7–9

Here are graphs A, B, C, D, E and F.

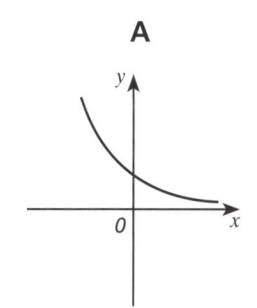

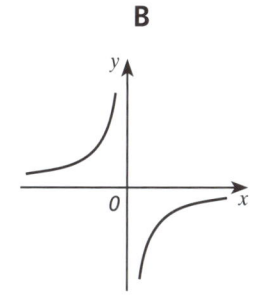

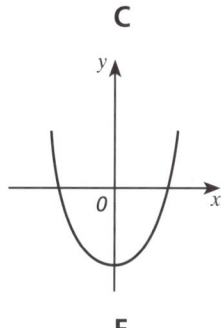

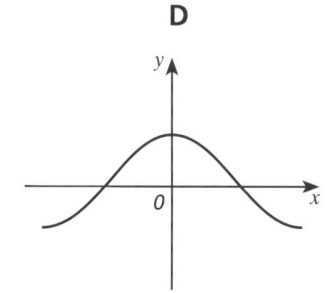

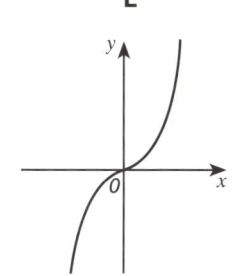

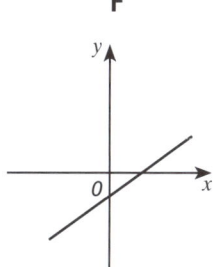

A B C

D E F

Match each equation with the corresponding graph.

Equation	Graph
$y = \cos x$	
$y = 2^{-x}$	
$y = 2x - 3$	
$y = -\dfrac{1}{x}$	
$y = x^2 - 3$	

(3)

Total score: ____ / 10

Complete

Worked example and more!

Fill in or add missing information to a statement, table or diagram.

TOP TIP
Double check that you have completed all rows and columns of tables correctly.

Example question

1 Probability • Grade 4–6

ξ = {odd numbers between 0 and 26}
A = {1, 3, 11, 13, 15}
B = {1, 15, 21, 23}
C = {3, 5, 7, 11, 15, 23, 25}

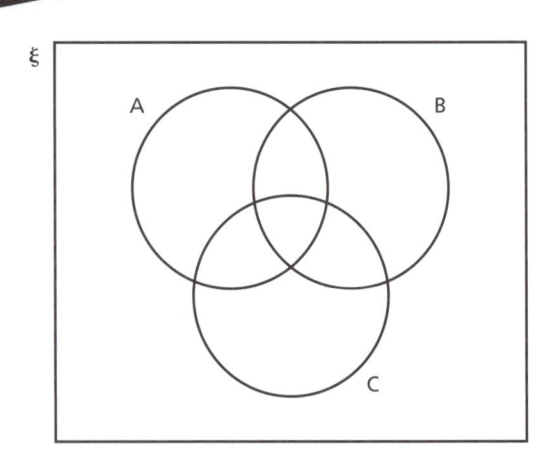

Complete the Venn diagram for this information. (4)

Complete the example

Statistics • Grade 4–6

Here is some information about the heights of 90 trees measured in metres.

Height, h (m)	$0 < h \leqslant 1$	$1 < h \leqslant 2$	$2 < h \leqslant 3$	$3 < h \leqslant 4$	$4 < h \leqslant 5$
Frequency	17	22	27	13	11

Complete the cumulative frequency table below. (1)

Height, h (m)	$\leqslant 1$	$\leqslant 2$	$\leqslant 3$	$\leqslant 4$	$\leqslant 5$
Frequency	17	39			

Exam practice questions

⏱ 20

1 Number • Grade 4–6

A number, n, is rounded to 1 decimal place.

The result is 67.5

Complete the error interval for n. (2)

$$67.45 \leqslant n < 67.55$$

2 Ratio, Proportion and Rates of Change • Grade 4–6

In a box are some squares, circles and triangles. Each shape is red or blue.
There are
- 43 red shapes
- 42 circles
- 12 blue squares.

The ratio of blue circles to red circles is 4 : 3

40% of the blue shapes are circles.

There is one more red square than there are blue squares.

Complete the two-way table. (4)

	Square	Circle	Triangle	Total
Blue	12	24	24	60
Red	13	18	12	43
Total	25	42	36	103

3 Statistics • Grade 4–6

The table below shows some information about the profit made each day by a café on 80 days.

Profit (£p)	Frequency
$0 < p \leq 150$	4
$150 < p \leq 300$	21
$300 < p \leq 450$	28
$450 < p \leq 600$	16
$600 < p \leq 750$	8
$750 < p \leq 900$	3

Complete the cumulative frequency table below for this information.

Profit (£p)	Frequency
$0 < p \leq 150$	
$0 < p \leq 300$	
$0 < p \leq 450$	
$0 < p \leq 600$	
$0 < p \leq 750$	
$0 < p \leq 900$	

(1)

4 Statistics • Grade 4–6

Avi recorded the heights of some plants.
He used his results to draw a box plot.

Heights of plants

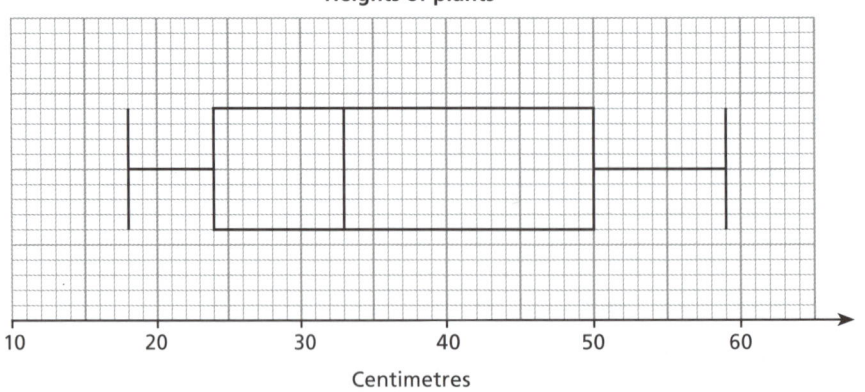

(box plot shown on axis from 10 to 60 Centimetres)

Complete the table below using the information from the box plot.

Least height	18 cm
Lower quartile	24 cm
Interquartile range	26 cm
Median	33 cm
Range	47 cm

(3)

5 Algebra • Grade 4–6

The table shows the nth term of four different sequences.

Complete the table. (4)

nth term	1st term	2nd term	5th term	10th term
$2n^2 - 2$	0	6	48	198
$4n + 1$	5	9	21	41
$\frac{1}{n}$	1	0.5	0.2	0.1
$7 - n^3$	6	−1	−118	−993

6 Statistics • Grade 7–9

The histogram represents the number of minutes that runners took to complete a park run.

The bar for $50 \text{ minutes} \leq t < 70 \text{ minutes}$ is missing.

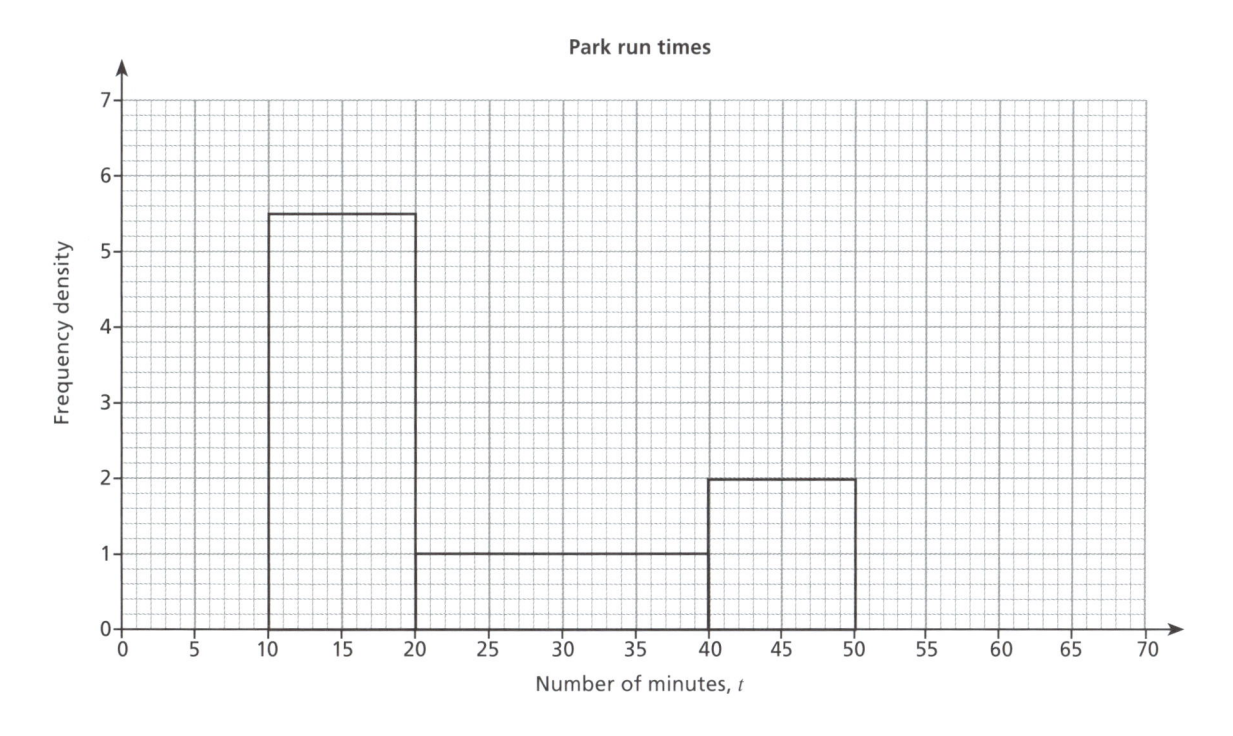

Altogether there are 105 runners.

Complete the histogram. (4)

7 Algebra • Grade 7–9

Complete the table of values for $y = 2^x + 1$

x	−2	−1	0	1	2	3
y	1.25			3		

(2)

Total score: ____ / 20

Estimate

Estimate a value from a graph: Read or interpret a value (it may be approximate) from a graph.

Estimate a probability: Use relative frequency to estimate a probability.

Estimate the value of a calculation: Round the numbers (usually to 1 significant figure) in a calculation to obtain an estimated answer.

Estimate a mean from a grouped frequency: Use the midpoints of the class intervals to calculate an approximate value of the mean.

Estimate a length: Use a scale drawing or map to estimate an actual distance.

Worked example and more!

TOP TIP
The symbol ≈ means 'approximately equal to'.

Example question

1 Number • Grade 4–6

Use approximations to *estimate* the value of $\dfrac{112 + 4.28^3}{0.52}$ (3)

Complete the example

Statistics • Grade 7–9

Here is a histogram showing speeds of cars on a road.

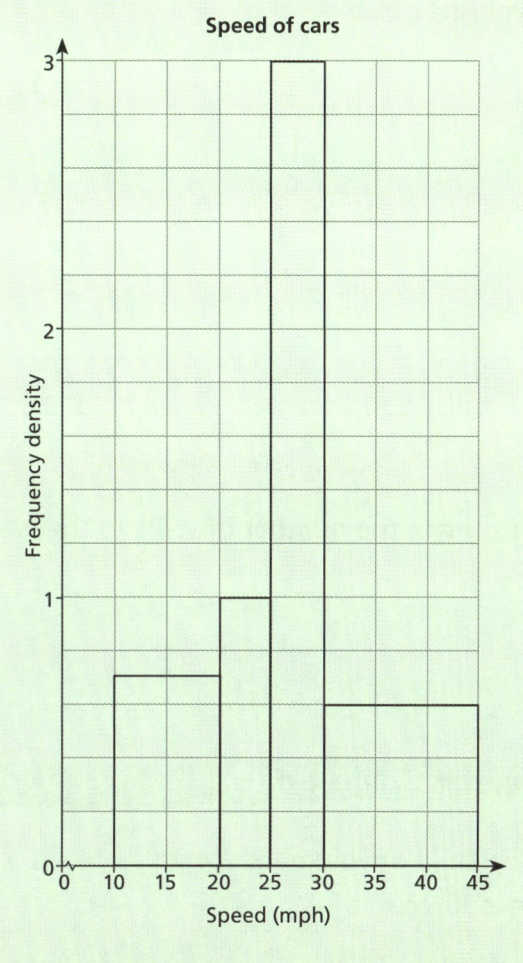

Use the graph to estimate the median speed. (4)

> Work out the frequency of each class interval and complete the table. To work out the frequency, multiply the class width by the frequency density.

Speed (s miles per hour)	Class width	Frequency density	Frequency	Cumulative frequency
$10 < s \leq 20$	10	0.7	7	7
$20 < s \leq 25$		1		
$25 < s \leq 30$		3		
$30 < s \leq 45$		0.6		

So the median lies in the interval ....

> Median divides the areas in half. Total area is 36, so half the area is 18.

Median = $25 + \frac{6}{15} \times 5$

= .... mph

> The median is the 18th value so it is the 6th out of 15 values in the interval.

Exam practice questions

1 Statistics • Grade 4–6

Here is some data about the amount of money a company spends on advertising and the number of visits to its website.

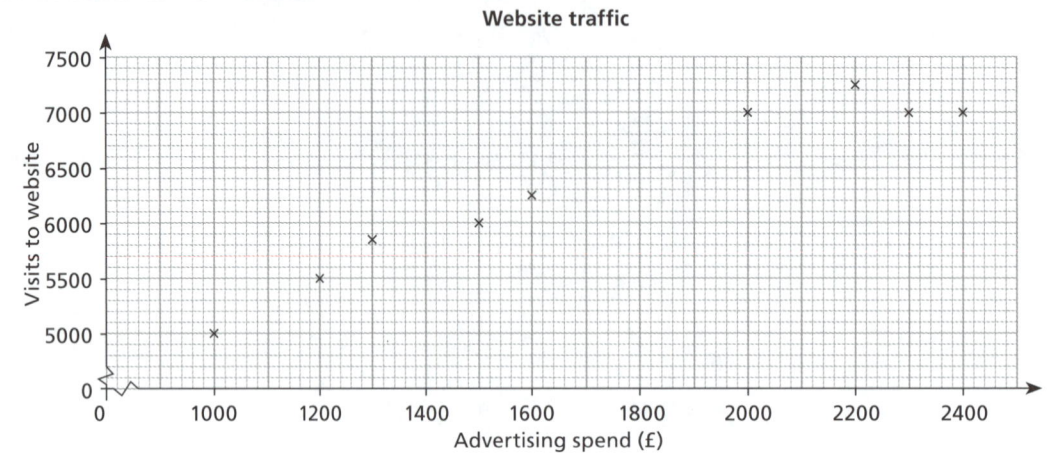

Website traffic

(Scatter graph with x-axis "Advertising spend (£)" from 0 to 2400, and y-axis "Visits to website" from 0 to 7500.)

Use a line of best fit to estimate the number of visits to the website if the company spends £1900 on advertising. (3)

2 Geometry and Measures • Grade 4–6

Here is a square-based pyramid of volume 812.4 cm³
Its perpendicular height is 30.2 cm

The formula for volume of a pyramid is $V = \frac{1}{3} \times$ base area $\times$ height

Use approximations to 2 significant figures to work out an estimate for the value of x.
You **must** show your working. (3)

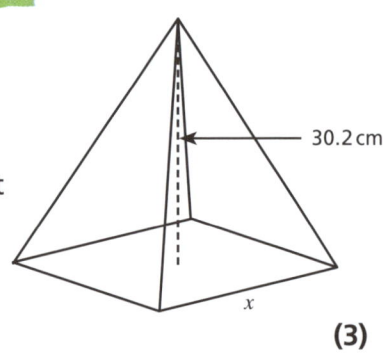

30.2 cm

$x =$ .... cm

3 Probability • Grade 4–6

Here is some data about the number of faulty mobile phones produced at a factory over 5 days.

Number of mobiles sampled	600	500	900	800	700
Number of faulty mobiles	54	48	99	82	84

Use the data to work out the best estimate for the probability that a phone chosen at random is faulty. (3)

4 Statistics • Grade 7–9

This cumulative frequency diagram shows data about the lengths of sea turtles in a bay.

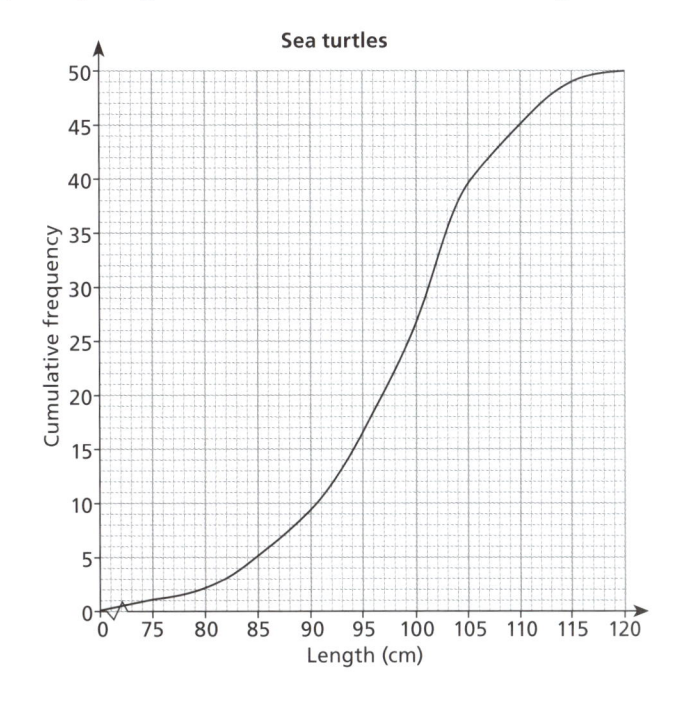

Estimate the median length of sea turtles in the bay. **(2)**

.... cm

5 Ratio, Proportion and Rates of Change • Grade 7–9

Here is a graph modelling the growth of bacteria in a petri dish.

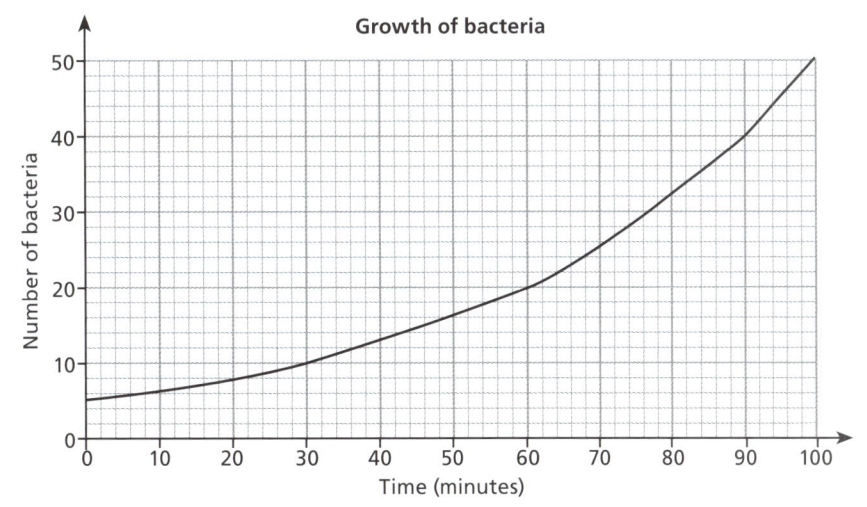

Estimate the rate of growth after 60 minutes.
Give your answer to 2 decimal places. **(3)**

.... bacteria per minute

Total score: .... / 14

Draw/Sketch

Worked examples and more!

Draw: Draw a graph or diagram accurately.

Sketch: Make an approximate drawing of a graph or diagram, showing the correct general shape with important points or distances labelled.

TOP TIP
Use a sharp pencil.

Example questions

1 Algebra • Grade 4–6

The table shows values for the equation $y = x^2 + x - 6$

x	–3	–2	–1	0	1	2
y	0	–4	–6	–6	–4	0

Draw a graph of the equation $y = x^2 + x - 6$ from $x = -3$ to $x = 2$ (2)

2 Algebra • Grade 7–9

The graph of $y = \sin x$ has been drawn on this grid.

On the grid, draw the graph of $y = -1 + \sin x$ for values of x from 0° to 360°.   (1)

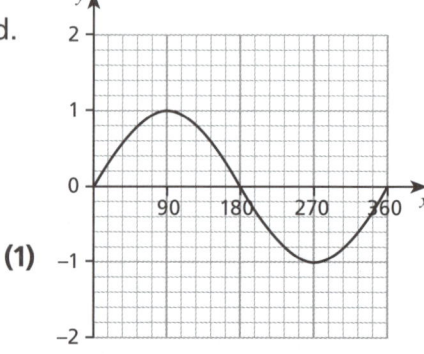

Complete the example

Statistics • Grade 7–9

A farmer samples the height of wheat in a field.
The table shows the results.

Height, x (cm)	Frequency
$40 \leq x < 50$	15
$50 \leq x < 65$	30
$65 \leq x < 75$	30
$75 \leq x < 80$	10

Draw a histogram to show the data. (3)

Add columns for class width and frequency density to the table.

Height, x (cm)	Frequency	Class width	Frequency density
$40 \leq x < 50$	15	10	15 ÷ 10 = 1.5
$50 \leq x < 65$	30	15	30 ÷ 15 = ...
$65 \leq x < 75$	30	....	.... ÷ 10 = ...
$75 \leq x < 80$	10	....	.... ÷ .... = ...

The height of the bars of a histogram is the frequency density. To work out the frequency densities for each class interval, divide the frequency by the class width interval.

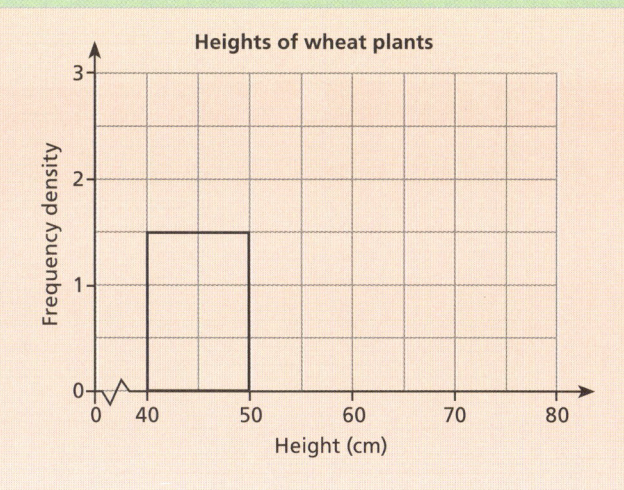

Heights of wheat plants

Exam practice questions

⏱ 20

1 Geometry and Measures • Grade 4–6

The diagram shows the plan, front elevation and side elevation of a solid shape, drawn on a centimetre grid.

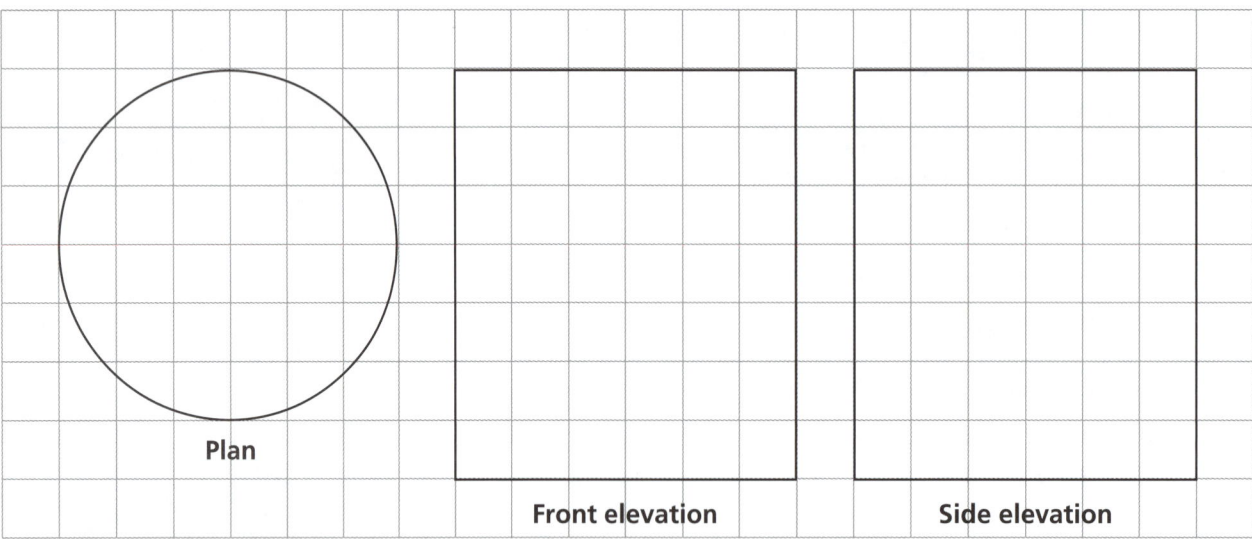

Plan

Front elevation

Side elevation

Draw a sketch of the solid shape.

Give the dimensions of the solid on your sketch. (2)

2 Geometry and Measures • Grade 4–6

Here is a triangle.

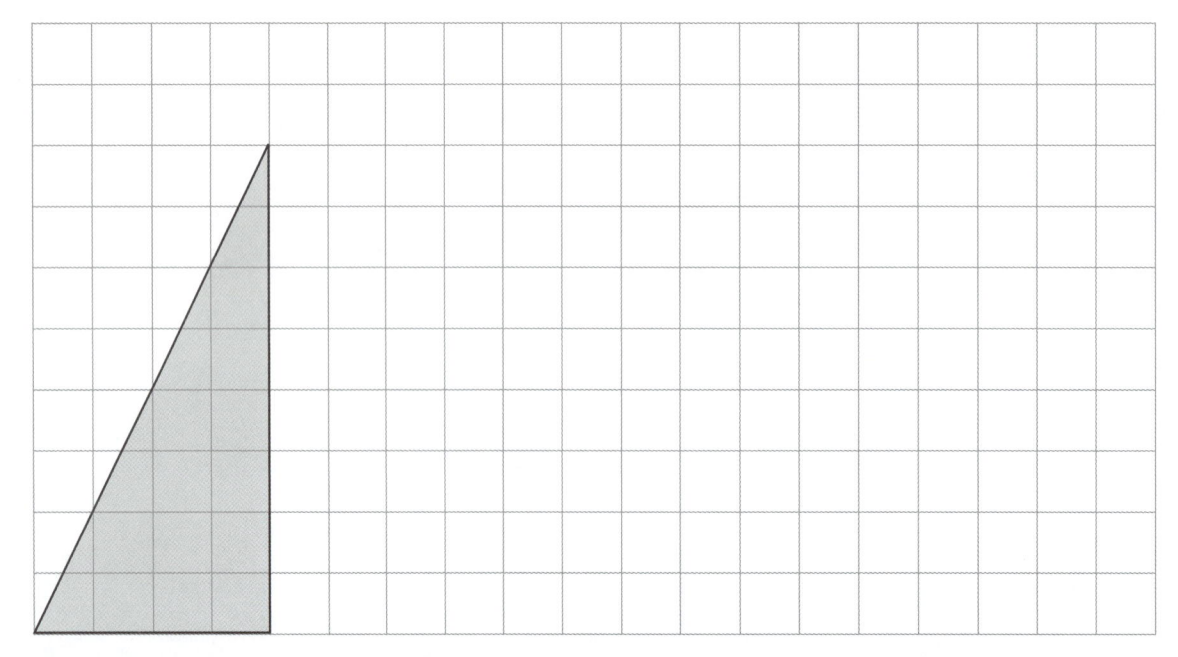

Draw an enlargement of the triangle using a scale factor of $\frac{3}{4}$ (2)

3 Ratio, Proportion and Rates of Change • Grade 4–6

Jenny drives from home to the shops at an average speed of 30 mph.
The journey takes 20 minutes.
She spends 30 minutes at the shops.
She then drives from the shops to a café at an average speed of 18 mph.
She arrives at the café 1 hour after leaving home.

Draw a distance–time graph to show this information. (3)

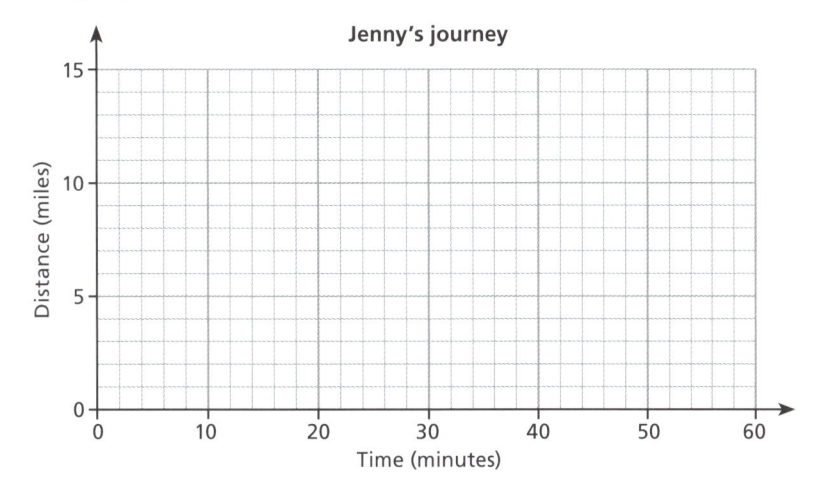

4 Algebra • Grade 4–6

Sketch the curve with equation $y = x^3 + 4$ (2)

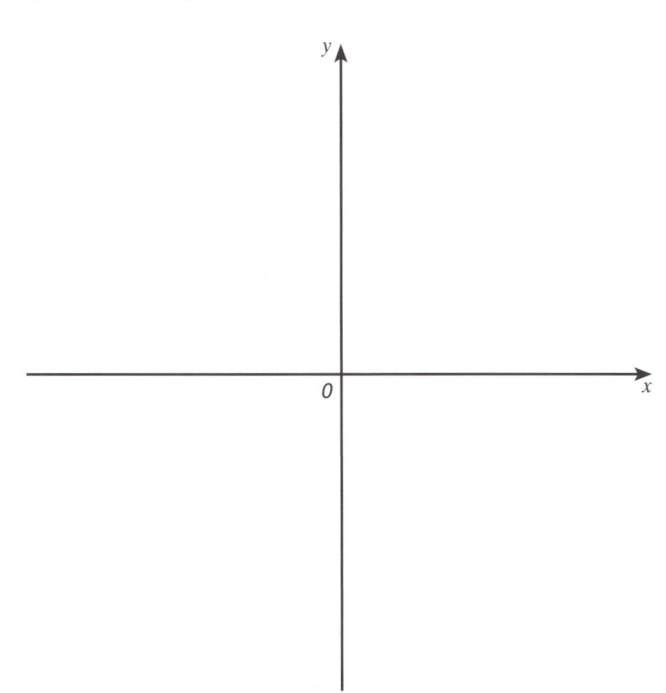

5 Statistics • Grade 4–6

Here is some data about the mass of some cats.

Mass, m (kg)	Number of cats
$3.0 < m \leq 3.5$	3
$3.5 < m \leq 4.0$	8
$4.0 < m \leq 4.5$	15
$4.5 < m \leq 5.0$	10
$5.0 < m \leq 5.5$	4

On the grid, draw a cumulative frequency graph. (3)

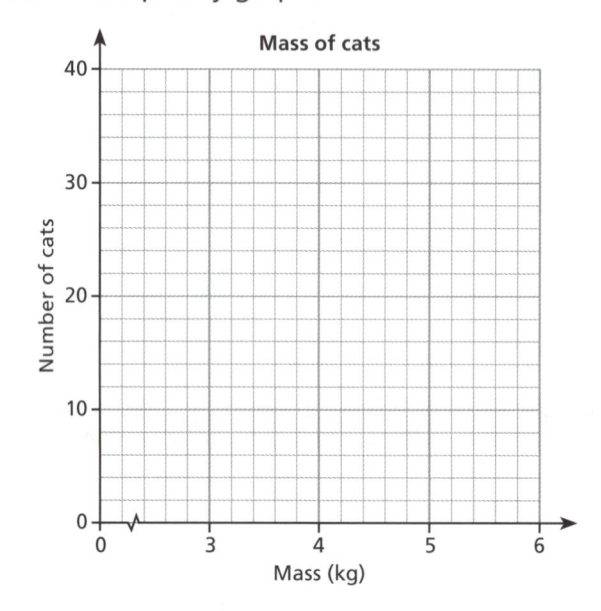

Mass of cats

6 Statistics • Grade 4–6

Here is data about the running times of some films at a cinema.

Longest film   152 minutes
Shortest film   94 minutes

Lower quartile   100 minutes
Upper quartile   140 minutes
Median time   125 minutes

Draw a box plot to show the data. (3)

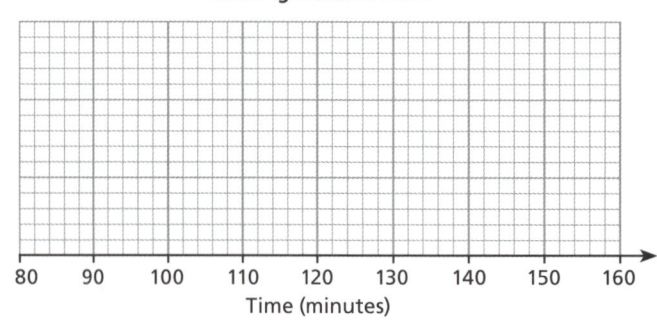

Running times of films

7 Algebra • Grade 7–9

Sketch the graph of $\quad x^2 + y^2 = 16$ (2)

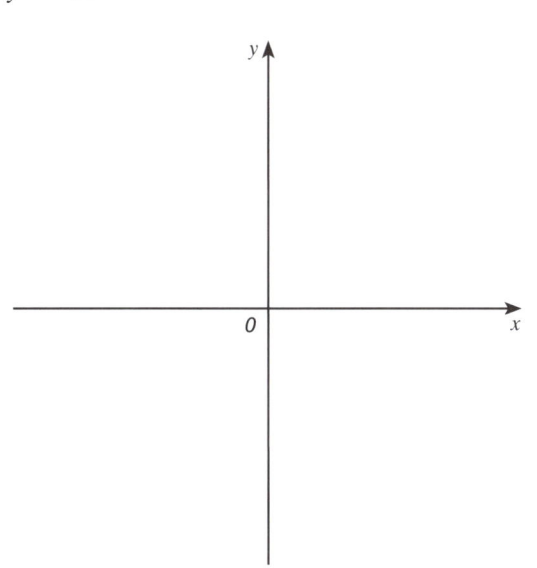

8 Algebra • Grade 7–9

$f(x) = 2x + 1 \quad$ and $\quad g(x) = x - 3$

Draw the graph of $\quad y = fg(x) \quad$ for values of x from 0 to 5 (2)

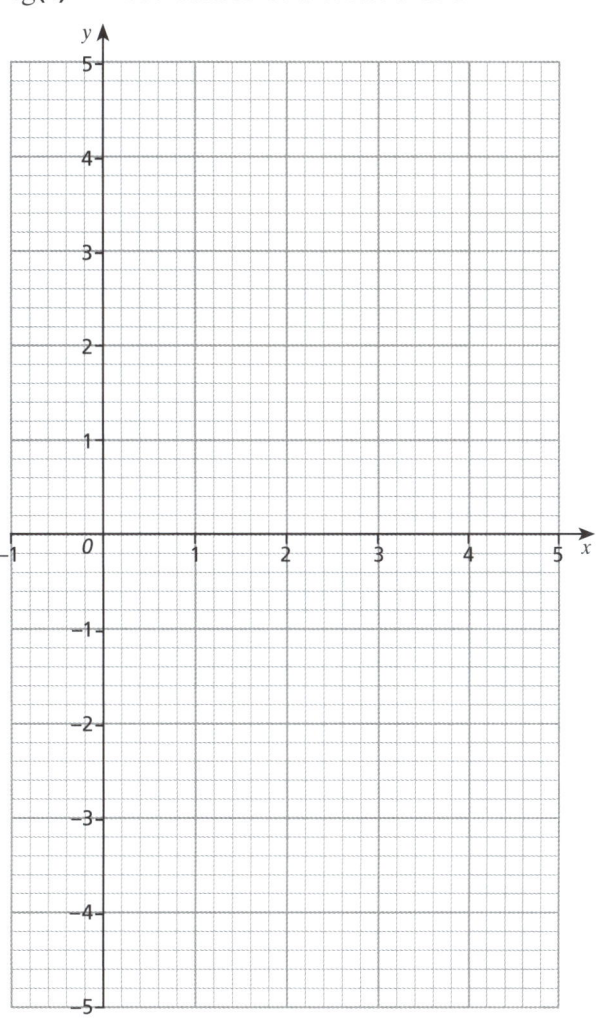

Total score: ...... / 19

Is ... correct?

Decide if a statement is correct and provide a reason. You must show working or give a reason for your answer. This could be working to show the correct answer, or it could be providing a reason or a counter-example.

Worked example and more!

TOP TIP
Tick any 'yes' or 'no' boxes as appropriate. If there aren't any boxes, state 'yes' or 'no' in your answer.

Example question

1 Geometry and Measures • Grade 4–6

Su is working out the three-figure bearing of A from B.

She writes,   Bearing = 100° + 120° = 220°

Is she correct?
Tick a box.

☐ Yes   ☐ No

Show working to support your answer.

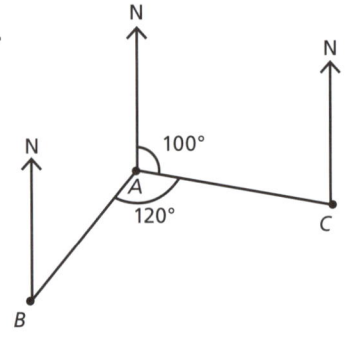

(1)

Complete the example

Statistics • Grade 7–9

The histogram shows information about the heights of 500 sunflowers on a farm.
The scale for the frequency density has been removed.

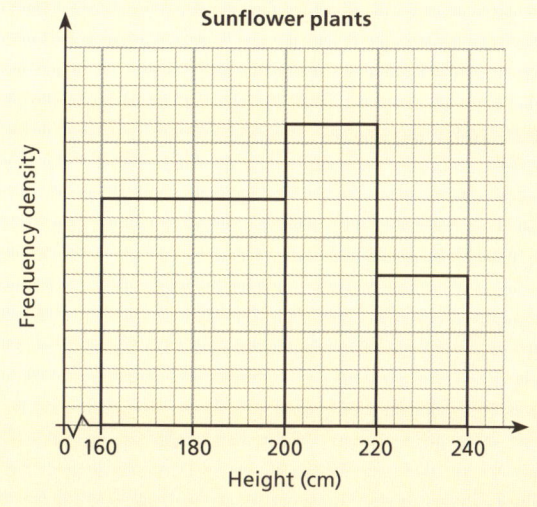

Craig says, "I can tell that most of the sunflowers are between 200 and 220 cm tall because the highest bar is between 200 and 220 cm."

Is he correct?

Show working to support your answer. (1)

> In the histogram, the areas of the bars show the frequencies. Use the small grid squares to work out the areas.

Area of the bar between 160 ≤ height < 200 cm is 12 × .... = ... square units

Area of the bar between 200 ≤ height < 220 cm is 16 × .... = ... square units

Area of the bar between 220 ≤ height < 240 cm is .... × 5 = ... square units

There are more sunflowers between .... cm ≤ height < .... cm

No, he is not correct.

Exam practice questions

1 Geometry and Measures • Grade 4–6

Arlo says these triangles are congruent.

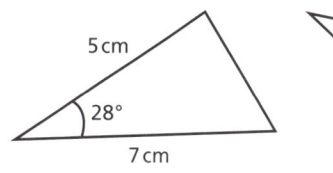

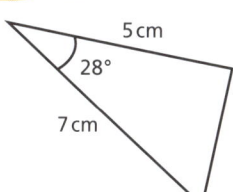

Is he correct?

Tick a box. ☑ Yes   ☐ No

Give a reason for your answer. (1)

SAS

2 Ratio, Proportion and Rates of Change • Grade 4–6

A drink is made by mixing juice with water in a ratio of 2 : 5

Ola has 100 ml of juice and 400 ml of water.

She says she can make a maximum of 350 ml of the drink.

Is she correct?

Tick a box. ☐ Yes   ☐ No

Show working to support your answer. (2)

3 Number • Grade 4–6

Ella says that $5^3 \times 5^6 = 5^{18}$

Is she correct?
Give a reason to support your answer. (1)

4 Statistics • Grade 7–9

This box plot shows a data set.

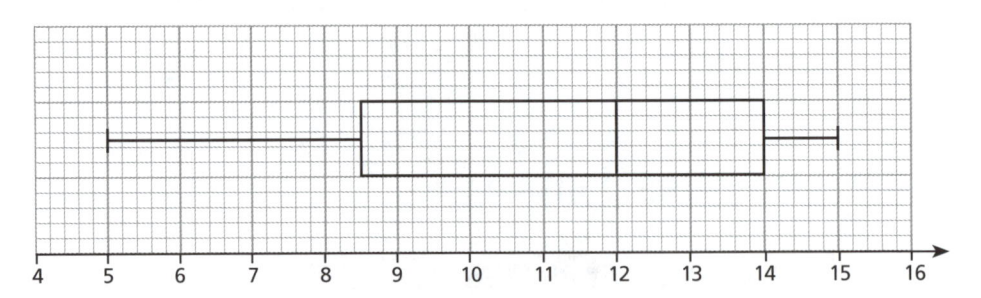

Omar says the interquartile range of the data set is 5.5

Is he correct?

Tick a box. ☐ Yes   ☐ No

Show working to support your answer. (1)

5 Number • Grade 7–9

Rupi says that $0.4\dot{5}$ cannot be written as a fraction.

Is she correct?
Show working to support your answer. **(2)**

6 Probability • Grade 7–9

A class has 30 students.

$\frac{2}{3}$ of the students study French.

40% of the students study Spanish.

4 students study French and Spanish.

A student is chosen at random from the class.
Vijay says the probability that this student studies Spanish given they study French is less than 25%.

Is he correct?
Show working to support your answer. You may use a Venn diagram to help you. **(3)**

7 Algebra • Grade 7–9

The equation of a curve is $y = x^2 - 10x + 28$
Isla says the turning point of the curve is where $x = -5$

Is she correct?

Tick a box. ☐ Yes ☐ No

You **must** show working to support your answer. **(3)**

Total score: ____ / 13

Use (a given method)

Use: A formula or fact may be given (e.g. a conversion) for you to use. You may be asked to use given data or a given graph to answer a question.

Use a given method (e.g. Pythagoras' theorem, complete the square): Use the stated method to find the answer.

Use approximations to: Round to 1 significant figure (unless told differently) and complete the calculation.

Use ruler and compasses: Construct the answer using a ruler and compasses, showing any construction arcs.

Worked example and more!

Use your calculator to: You can use your calculator to work out the answer in one step (but it is advisable to show any intermediate steps of working).

TOP TIP
Don't use another method unless the question says 'or otherwise'.

Example question

1 Geometry and Measures • Grade 4–6

Use trigonometry to work out the size of angle x.
Give your angle to the nearest degree.

(2)

3 cm, 5 cm, x

Complete the example

Ratio, Proportion and Rates of Change • Grade 7–9

Here is a graph of the path of a football after a goalkeeper kicks it in the air.

Use the graph to work out the speed of the ball at 2 seconds. (3)

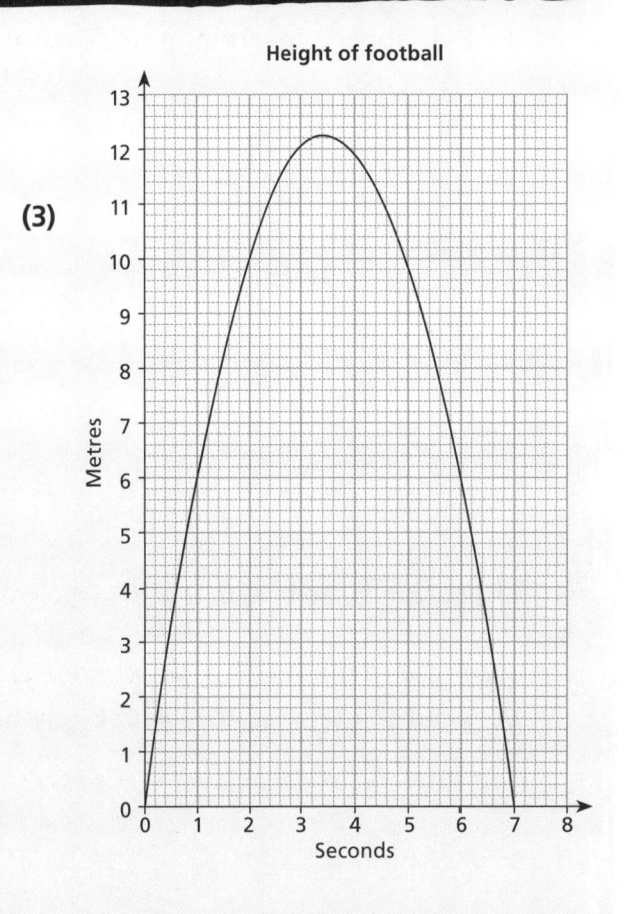

To work out the speed at 2 seconds, draw the .... to the curve at $x = $ ....

Then work out the gradient of the tangent. Make a right-angled triangle.

Points (0, ...) and (2, ...) are on the tangent.

$$\frac{\text{............} - \text{............}}{\text{............} - \text{............}} = \frac{6}{2} = 3$$

The speed is .... m/s.

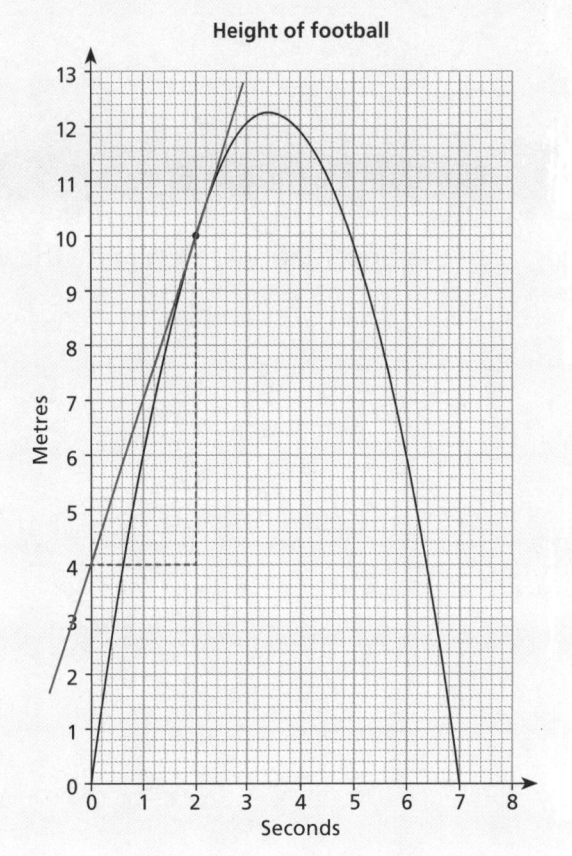

Exam practice questions

25

1 Geometry and Measures • Grade 4–6

Use Pythagoras' theorem to work out the height, h, of triangle ABC. **(2)**

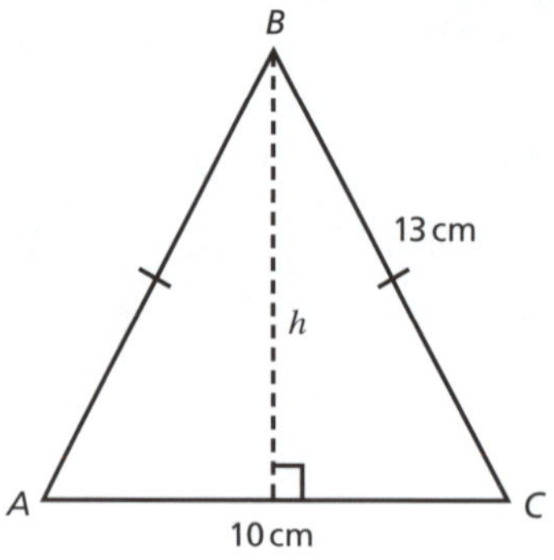

h = 12 cm

2 Algebra • Grade 4–6

Use the formula $F = \frac{9}{5}C + 32$, where F is degrees Fahrenheit and C is degrees Celsius, to work out the temperature in Celsius when it is 100°F. **(2)**

.... °C

3 Number • Grade 4–6

Use approximations to estimate the value of $\dfrac{\sqrt{102} - 3.068^2}{0.51 + 2.8}$ **(3)**

....

4 Statistics • Grade 4–6

This scatter graph shows the correlation between the temperature and the number of visitors to a beach.

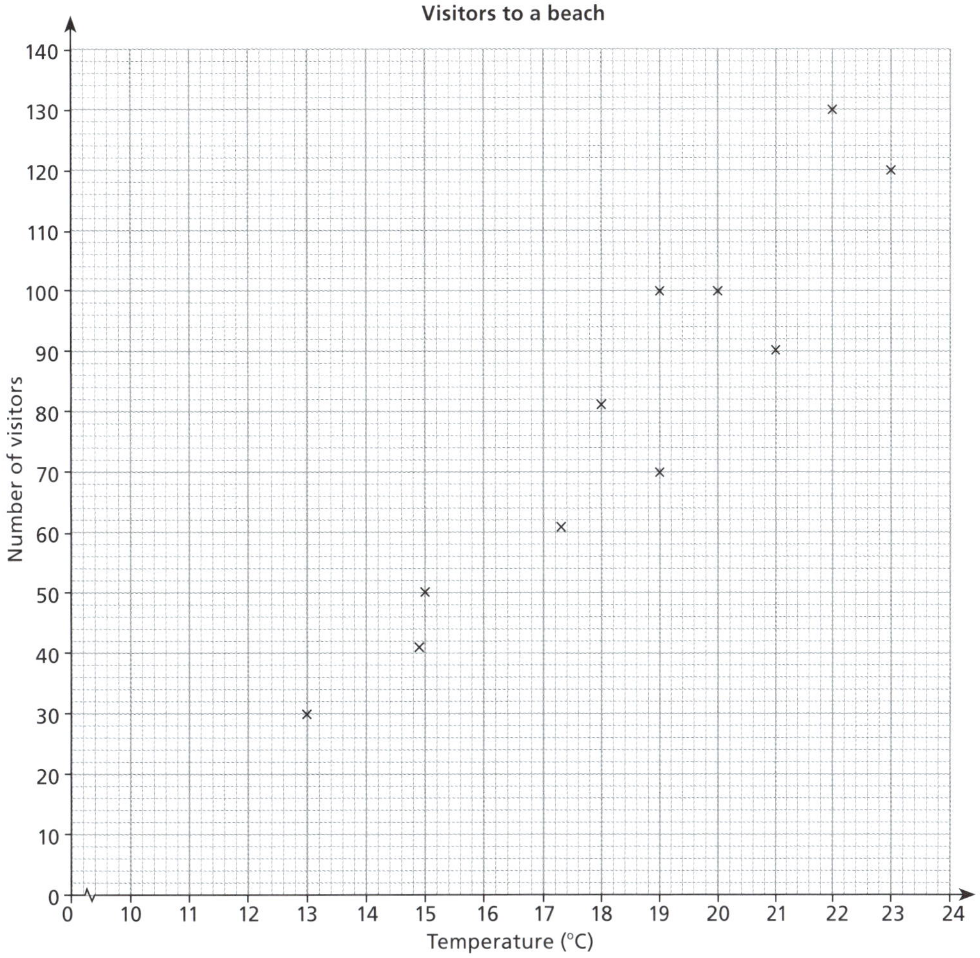

Use a line of best fit to predict the number of visitors to the beach when the temperature is 16°C **(2)**

....

5 Probability • Grade 4–6

A bag contains 7 red marbles and 3 green marbles.
Two marbles are taken from the bag at random and **not** replaced.

Use a tree diagram or another method to work out the probability that a green marble and a red marble are taken from the bag. **(3)**

....

6 Statistics • Grade 4–6

Here is a cumulative frequency graph representing barbecue sales each month for a year.

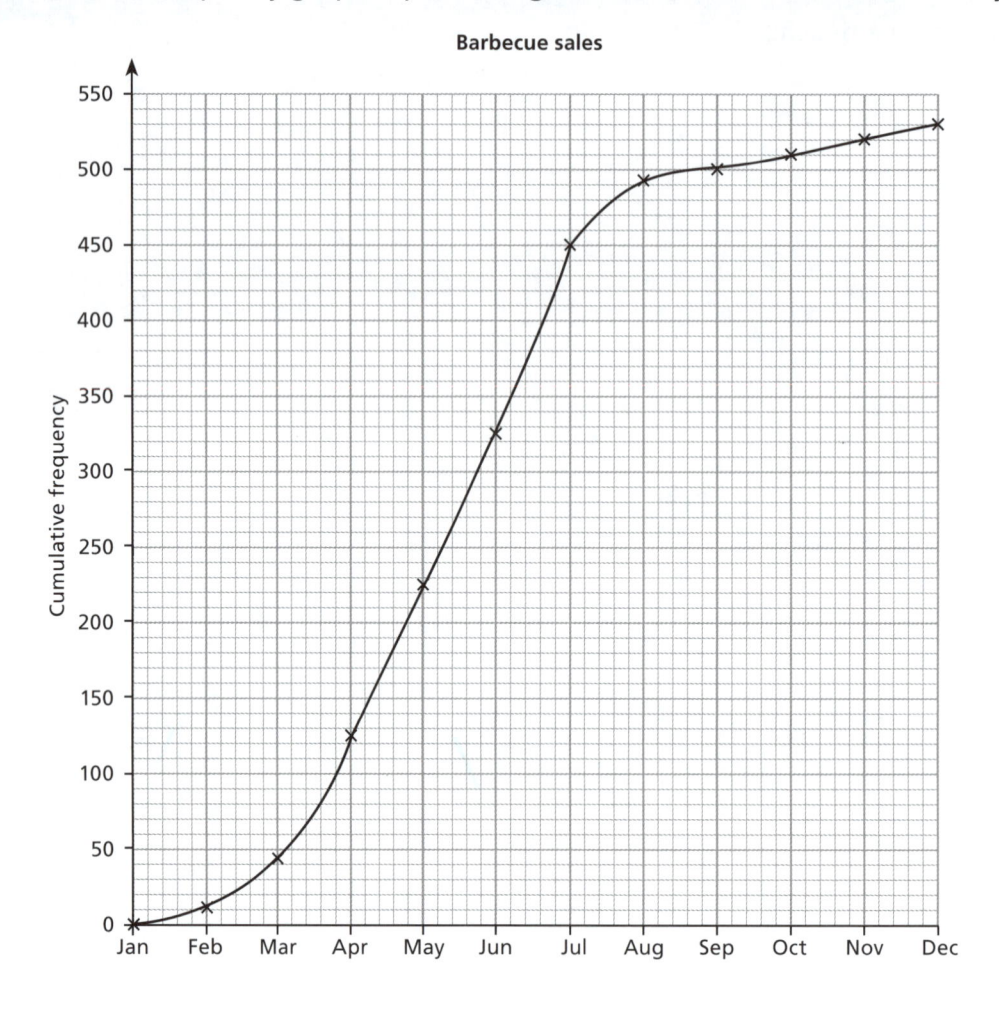

Use the graph to estimate the proportion of barbecues sold from the end of April to the end of September. **(2)**

....

7 Geometry and Measures • Grade 7–9

Use the sine rule to work out the size of angle x.
Give your answer to the nearest degree. **(3)**

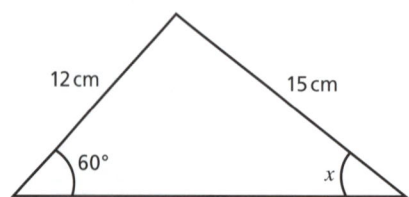

$x = $ ....°

8 Algebra • Grade 7–9

A straight line has equation $y = -4x - 4$
A curve has the equation $y = 4x^2 + 8x + 5$

Use an algebraic method to show that the line and the curve intersect at exactly one point.   (4)

9 Algebra • Grade 7–9

Use the method of completing the square to solve the quadratic equation

$$x^2 - 8x + 5 = 0$$

Give your answer in the form $a \pm \sqrt{b}$ where a and b are integers.   (4)

Total score: / 25

Translate/Reflect/Rotate/Enlarge

Translate: Draw the image in the correct position.

Reflect: Draw the mirror image of the object in the correct position.

Enlarge: Using the given scale factor, draw the image at the correct size. The image must also be in the correct position if you are given a centre of enlargement on a coordinate grid.

Rotate: Draw the image in the correct position and orientation.

Worked example and more!

Example question

1 Geometry and Measures • Grade 4–6

Rotate the shape 90° clockwise about the point (4, 3). **(2)**

TOP TIP
Use a ruler to draw the image accurately.

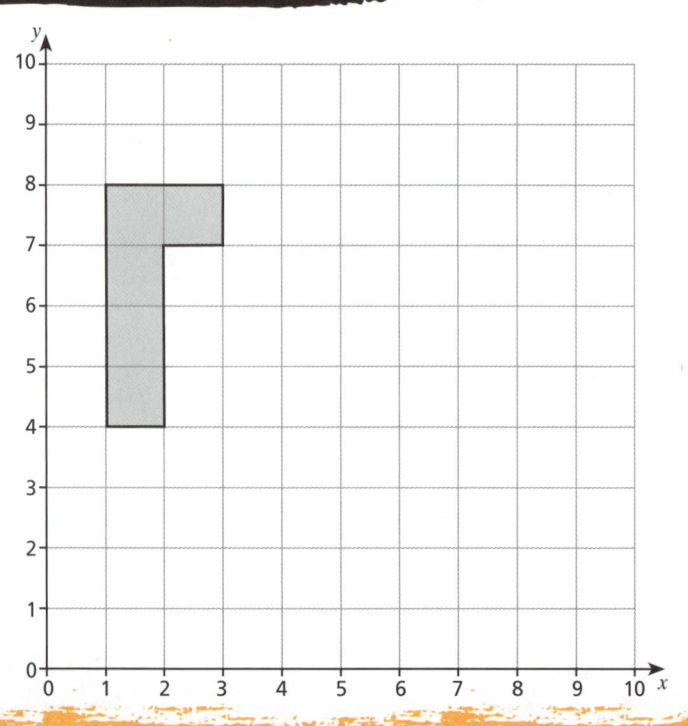

Complete the example

Geometry and Measures • Grade 4–6

Enlarge the triangle by a scale factor of $\frac{1}{2}$ about centre (0, 0). (2)

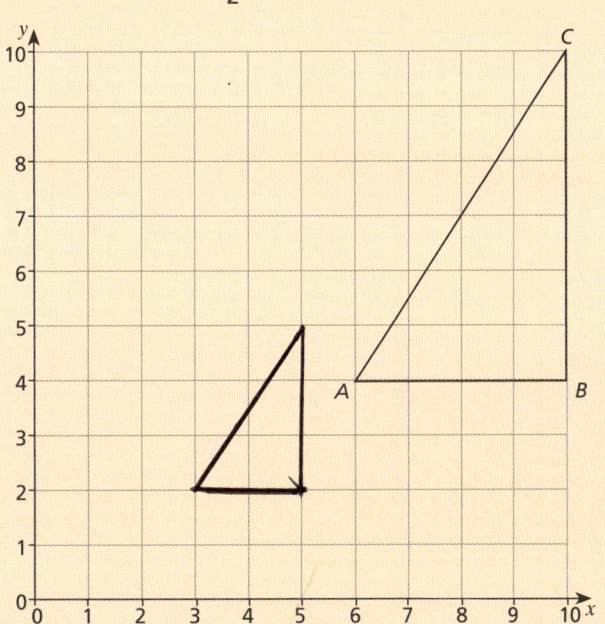

Follow these steps:
- Draw ray lines from each vertex to the centre of enlargement.
- Find the distance of each vertex in the x- and y-direction from the centre of enlargement.
- The distance from the origin to A is 6 in the x-direction and 4 in the y-direction, or $\binom{6}{4}$, so the distance from the origin to A' (the new point) is $\binom{3}{2}$.
- Plot the point (3, 2).
- Repeat for the other vertices.
- Join the new points to form the image.

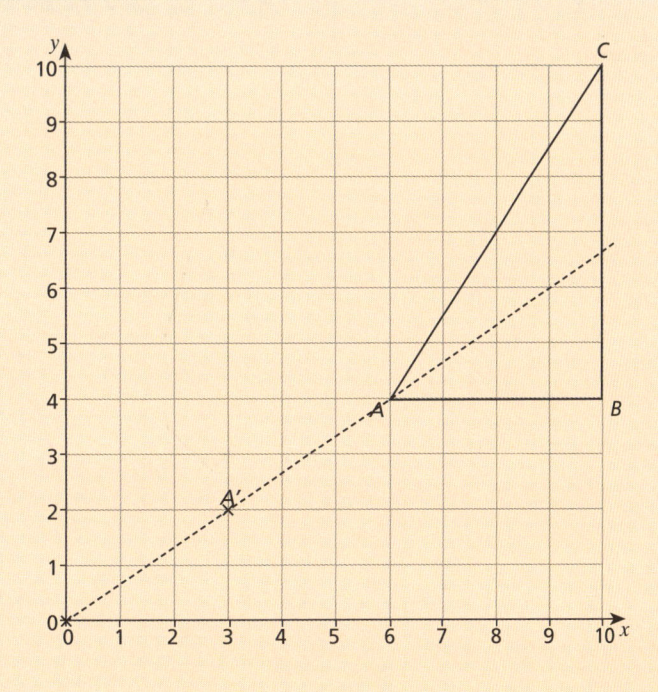

Exam practice questions

1 **Geometry and Measures • Grade 4–6**

Reflect the trapezium in the line $x = 4$ (2)

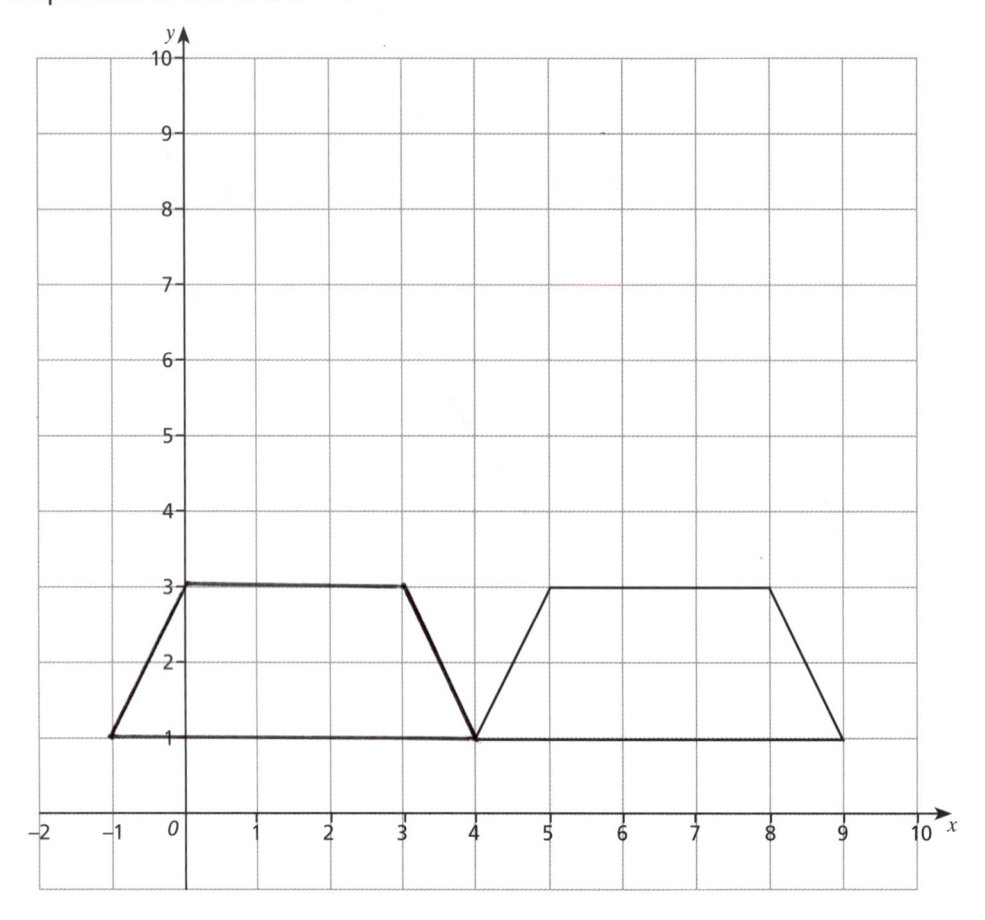

2 **Geometry and Measures • Grade 4–6**

Translate the quadrilateral by $\begin{pmatrix} -3 \\ 2 \end{pmatrix}$ (2)

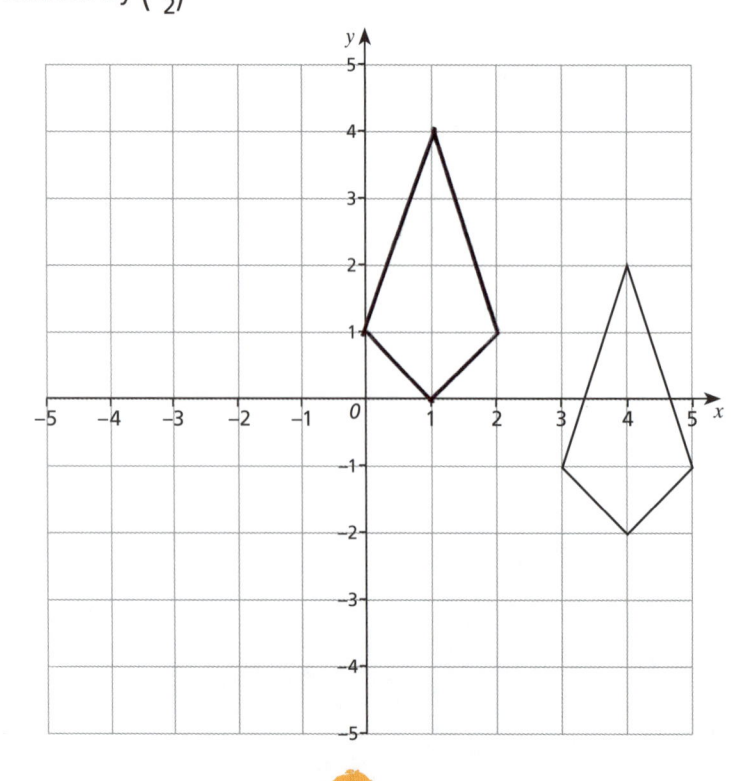

3 Geometry and Measures • Grade 7–9

Reflect the pentagon in the line $y = -x$ (2)

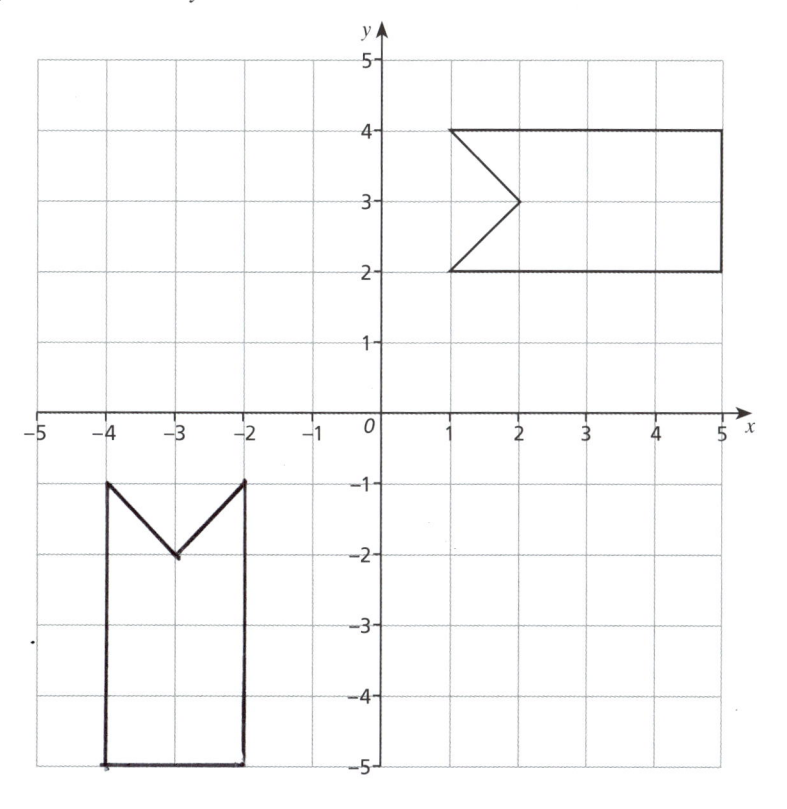

4 Geometry and Measures • Grade 7–9

Enlarge the triangle by a scale factor of −2 about centre (1, 2). (2)

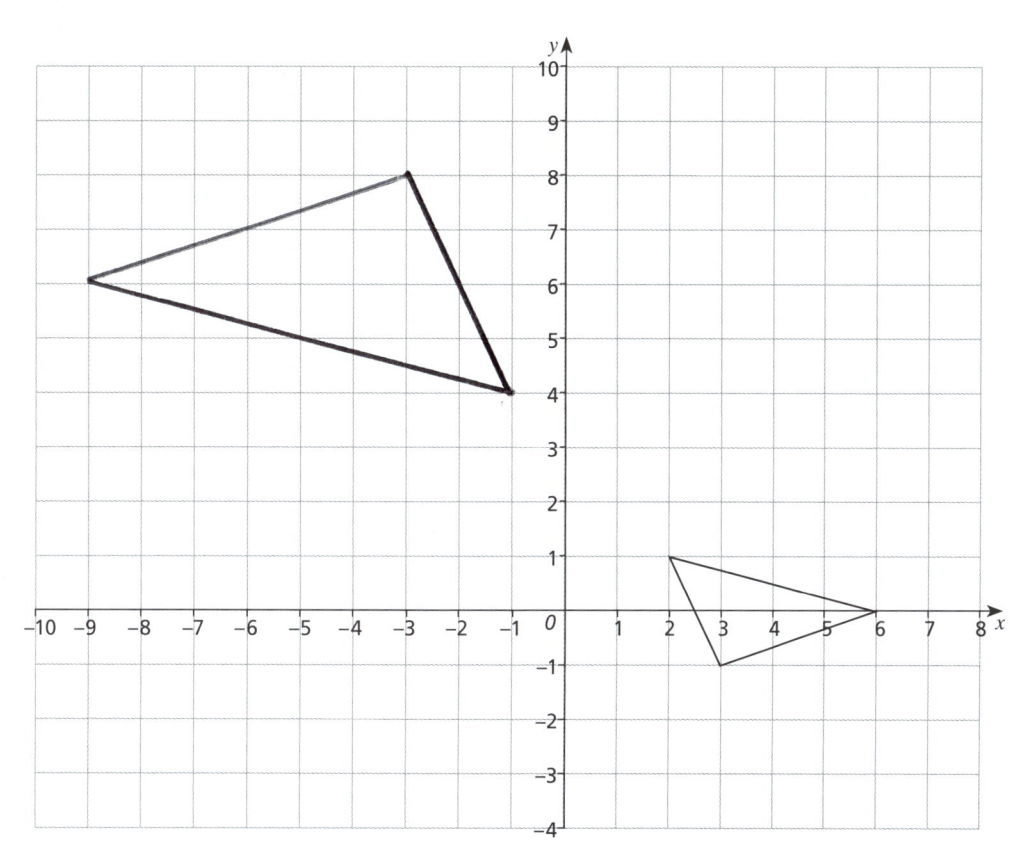

Total score: ___ / 8

Describe

Worked example and more!

Describe: Use mathematical words to describe, define or explain a given diagram, pattern or sequence.

Describe (fully) the single transformation that maps: Use mathematical words to state what single transformation has changed a shape on a coordinate grid.

TOP TIP
'Describe fully' is a reminder that there is more than one part to the answer.

Example question

1 Algebra • Grade 4–6

Here is a sequence.

0   6   14   24   36

a) Describe a rule for continuing the sequence. (1)

b) Describe the type of sequence. (1)

Complete the example

Geometry and Measures • Grade 7–9

Here is a kite, ABCD.

The kite undergoes a single transformation such that
- Point A moves to (9, 4)
- Point B moves to (7, 6)
- Point C is invariant
- Point D moves to (7, 1)

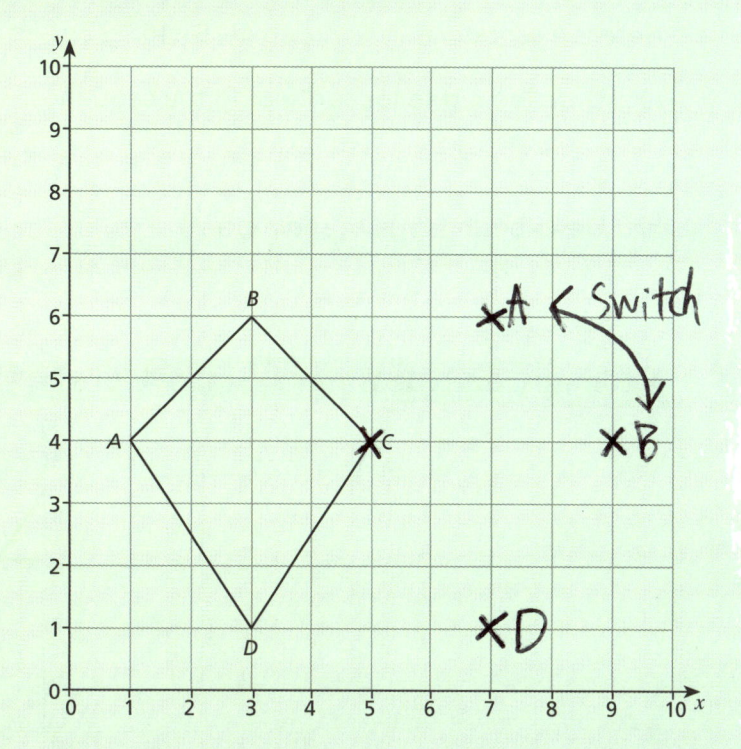

(Annotations on graph: ×A ← Switch, ×B, ×D)

Describe fully the single transformation. Reflection in the line $x=5$ (2)

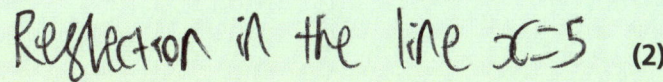

Plot the given points to visualise the transformation.

You can tell the kite has been reflected because it is a mirror image. Work out the midpoint between corresponding points to find the line of reflection.

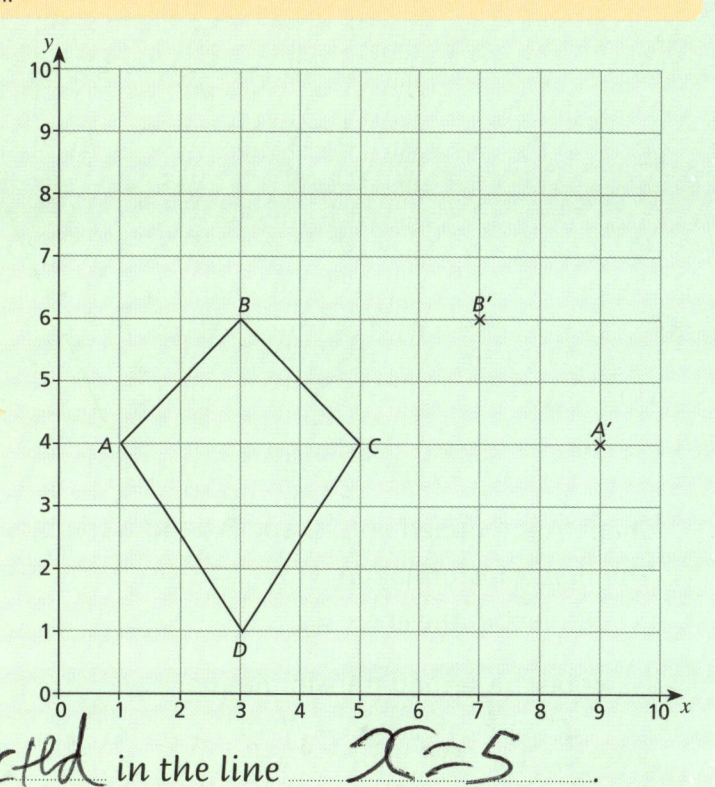

Kite ABCD has been **reflected** in the line $x=5$.

There may be more than one correct answer. In this case, ABCD could also have undergone an enlargement with a scale factor of –1 from the point (5, 4).

Exam practice questions

1 Algebra • Grade 4–6

Here is a sequence.   2 4 8 16 32

a) Describe a rule for continuing the sequence. (1)

Double the number each number increases by

b) Describe the type of sequence. (1)

2 Geometry and Measures • Grade 4–6

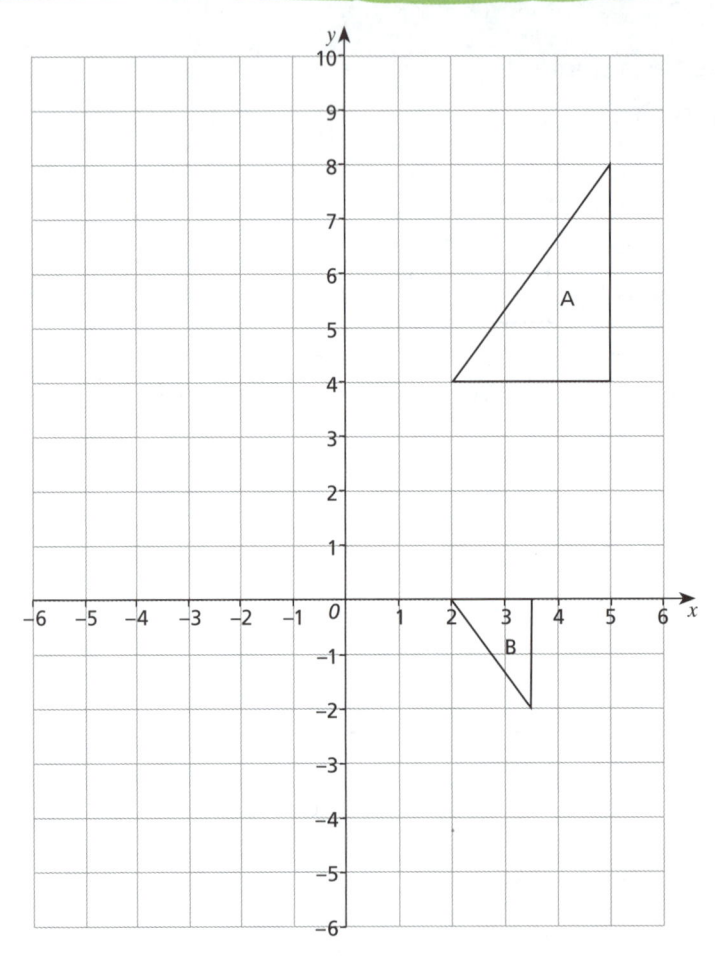

Shape A is mapped onto shape B using a combination of two transformations.

The first transformation is

   Reflect in the line $y = 2$

Describe the second transformation. (3)

Enlargement by scale factor $\frac{1}{2}$ with centre of enlargement (2,0)

3 Algebra / Geometry and Measures • Grade 4–6

For a regular polygon, with exterior angle x

$$x = \frac{360}{k}$$

Describe what k represents. (1)

....

4 Algebra • Grade 4–6

$$y = \frac{5}{x^2}$$

Describe what happens to the value of y as the value of x is doubled. (1)

....

....

5 Statistics • Grade 7–9

Sinead recorded the number of tulips in front gardens on her road.
This box plot shows her results.

Tulips in front gardens

Number of tulips

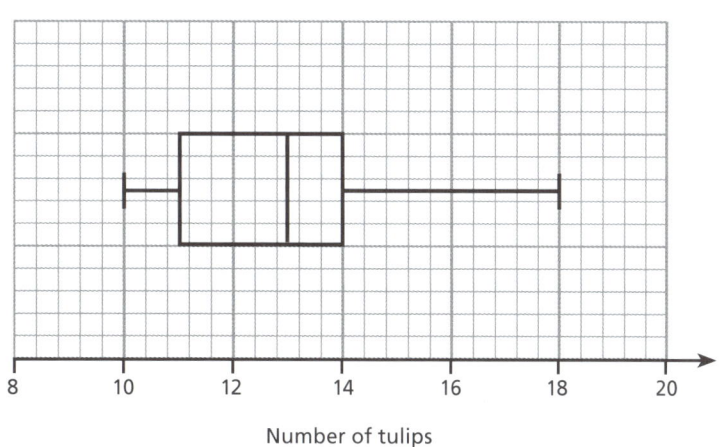

Describe the distribution of tulips. (2)

....

....

6 Algebra • Grade 7–9

Here is a graph showing $y = x^2 - x - 2$ and $y = 5$

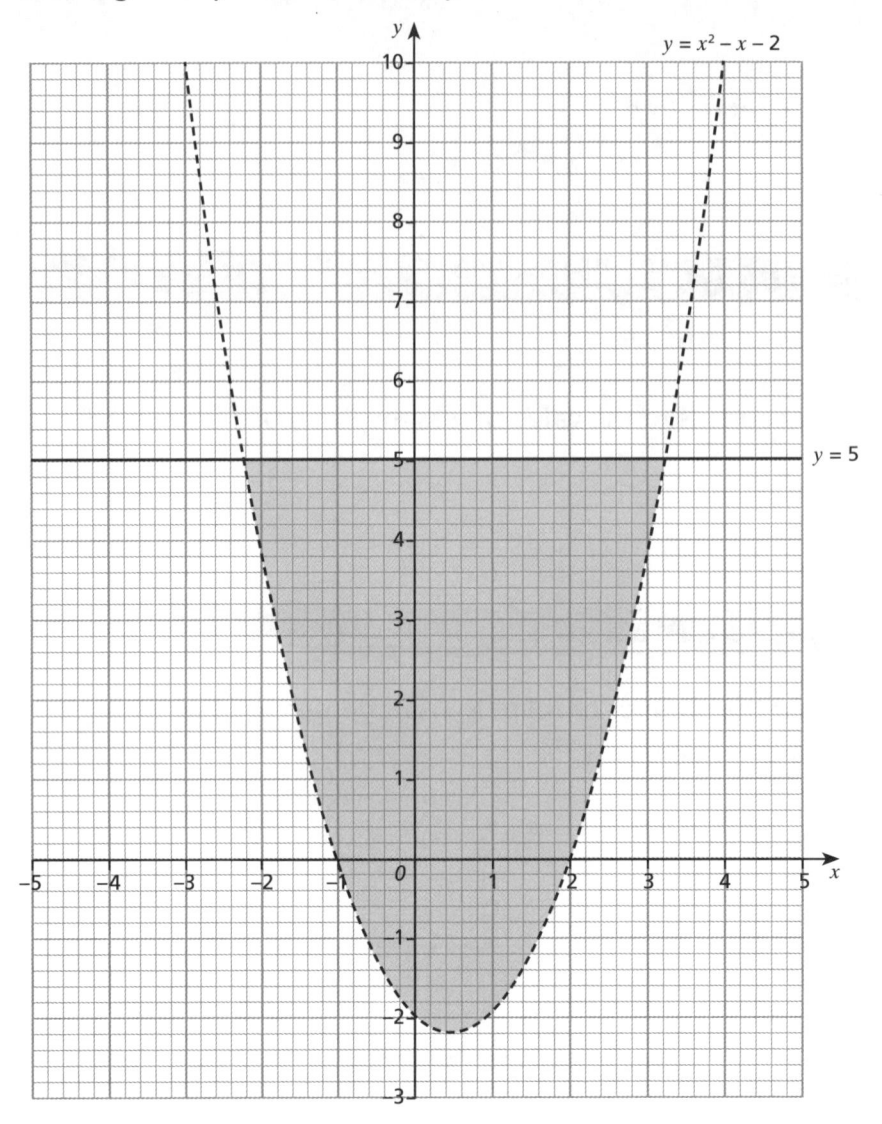

Use inequalities to describe the shaded region. (2)

7 Algebra • Grade 7–9

The graphs of $y = f(x)$ and $y = g(x)$ are shown.

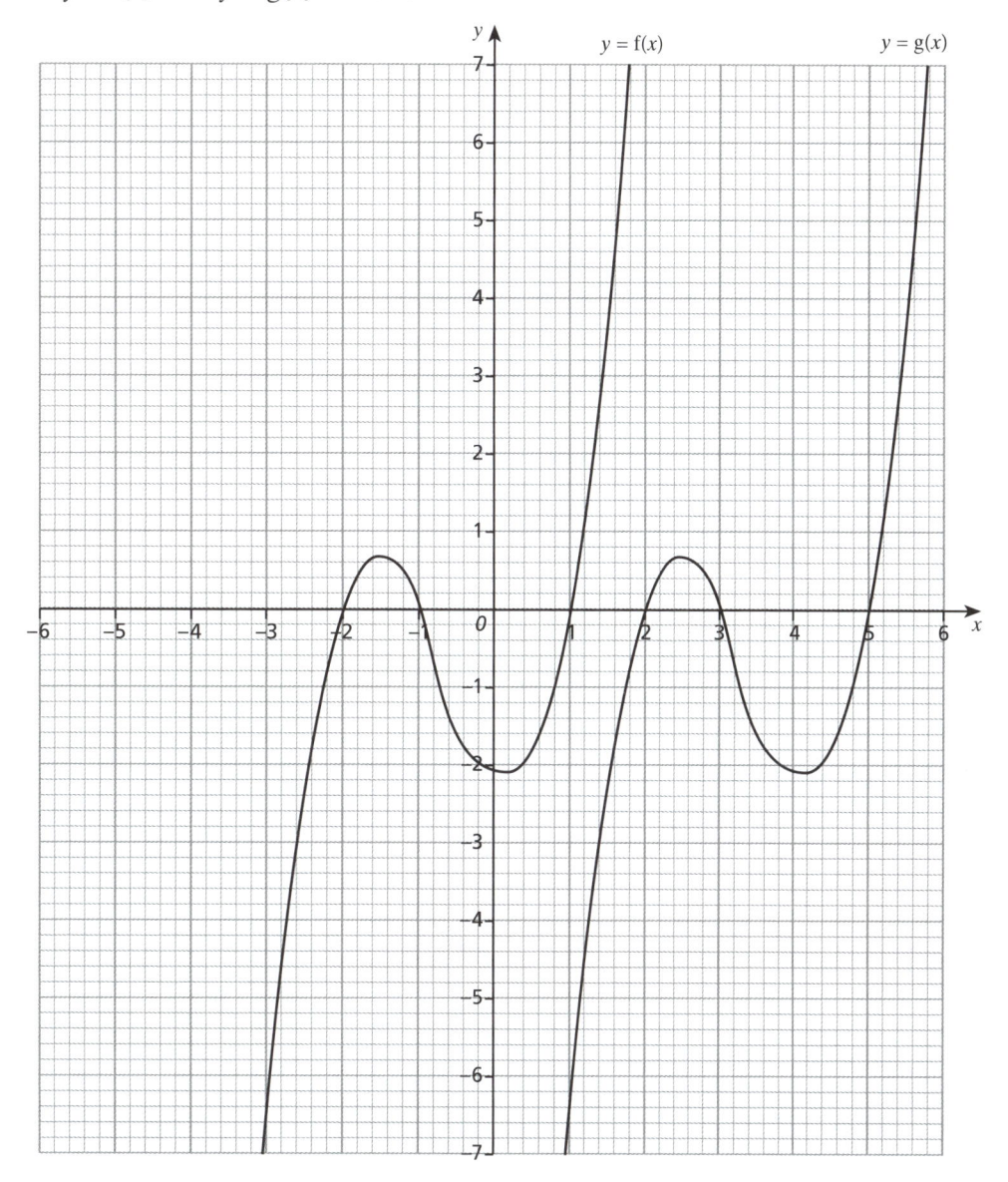

Describe **fully** the transformation of $y = f(x)$ to $y = g(x)$ (2)

....

....

Total score: .... / 13

Construct

Worked examples and more!

Construct / Show your construction lines: Draw accurately using ruler and compasses.

TOP TIP Remember to show all your construction lines and arcs, and make sure they are clear.

Example questions

1 Geometry and Measures • Grade 4–6

A triangular field has side lengths of 20 m, 24 m and 28 m

Construct a drawing of the field using a scale of 4 m = 1 cm (3)

2 Geometry and Measures • Grade 4–6

Using ruler and compasses, construct the perpendicular bisector of AB. (2)

A
      B

Complete the example

Geometry and Measures • Grade 4–6

Here is a map of a park.

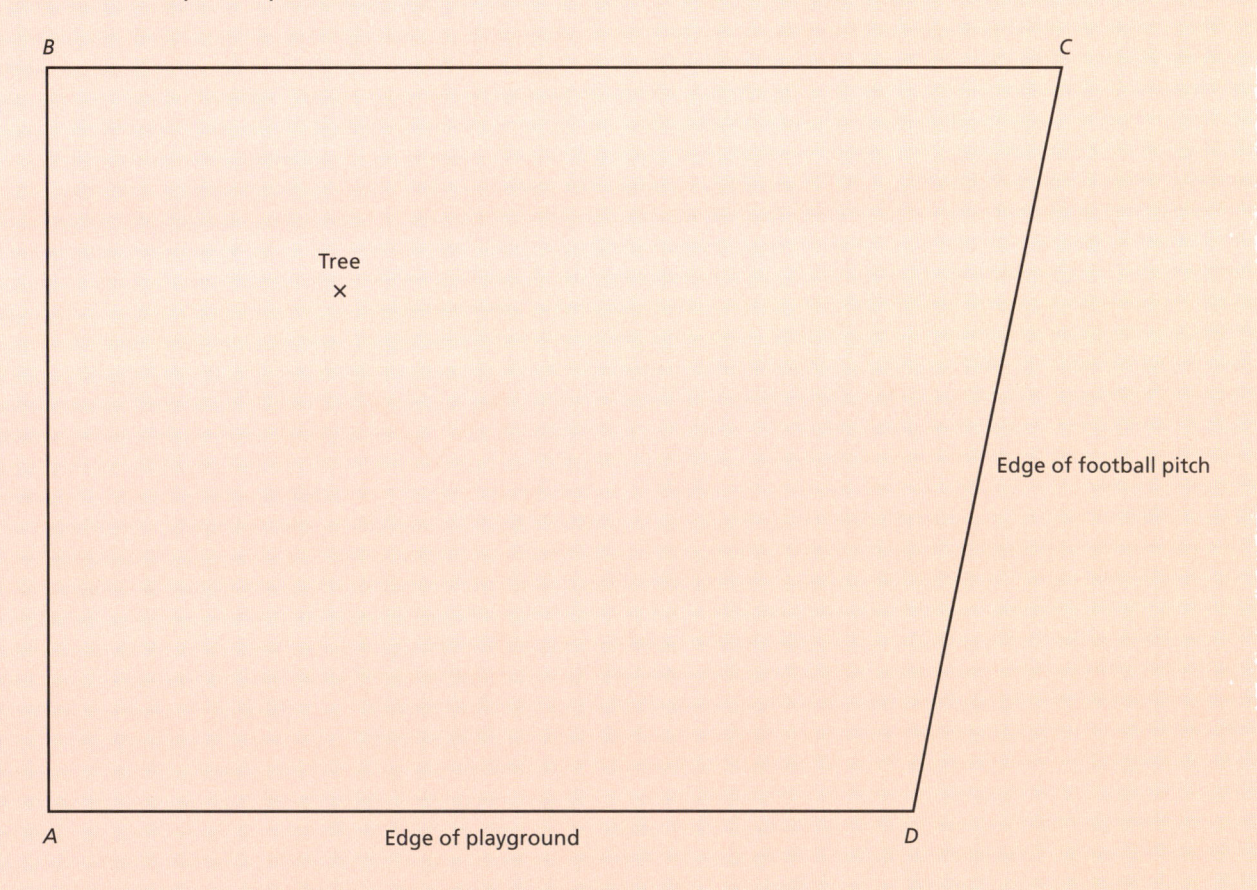

B ─────────────────────── C

   × Tree

                          Edge of football pitch

A ─── Edge of playground ─── D

There is an ice cream stand in the park.

- It is more than 20 metres from the tree.
- It is closer to the playground than to the football pitch.

Construct the region R to show where the ice cream stand could be.

Use a scale of 1 cm to 5 m. (3)

Complete the example (cont.)

Using the scale of 1 cm to 5 m, 20 m is .... cm on the map.

Draw a circle with radius of .... cm around the tree.

To identify the area that is nearer to the playground than the football pitch, construct the .... of angle ADC.

Label the region .... the circle and to the left of the .... as R.

> To construct the angle bisector:
> Put the point of the compasses on the vertex of the angle and draw an arc on both lines of the angle.
> Put the point of the compasses on the intersection of the arc and one line of the angle and draw an arc in the centre of the angle. Make an equal sized arc using the other point of intersection.
> Draw a line through the vertex and the point of intersection of the arcs.

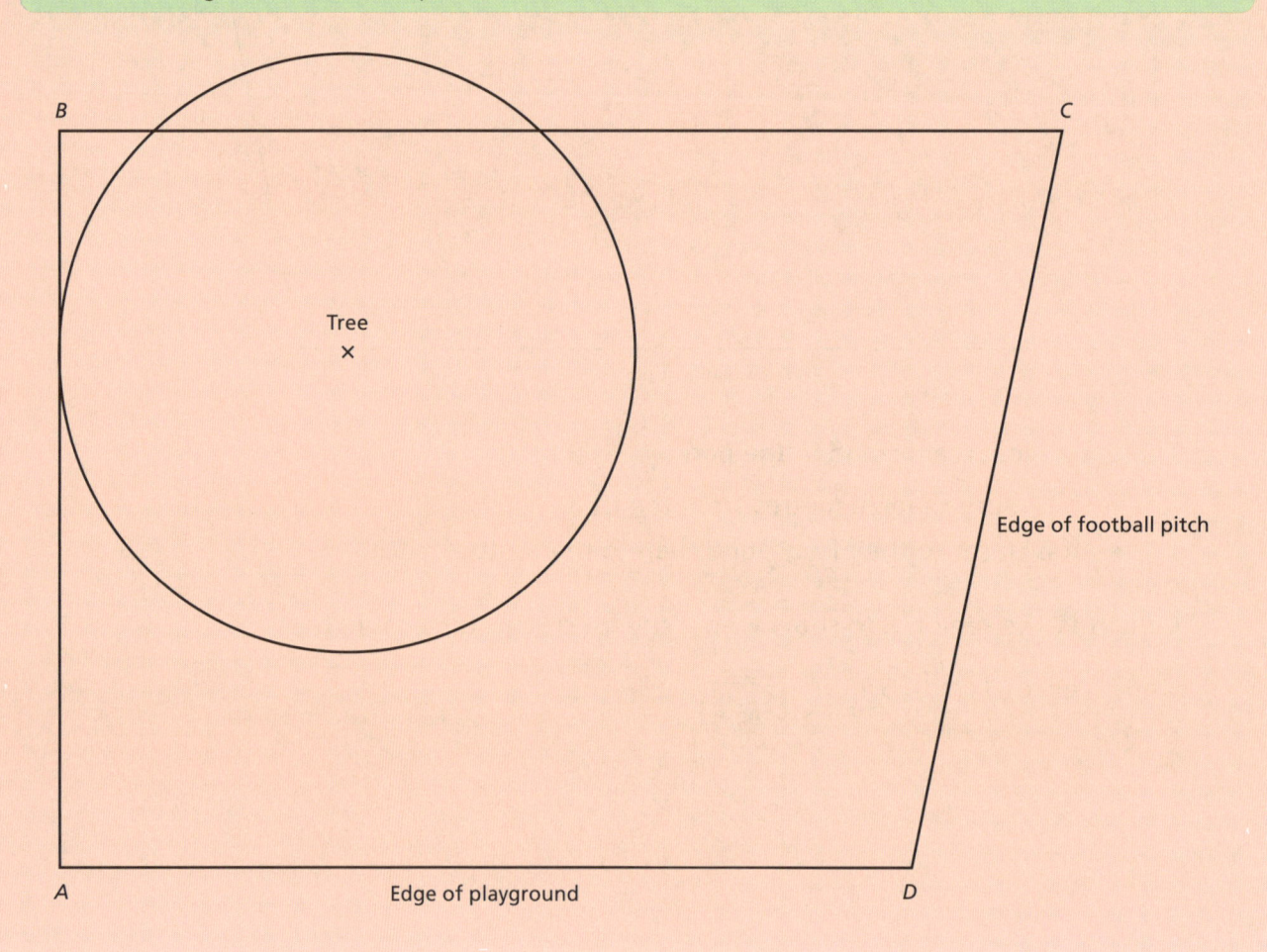

Exam practice questions

1 Geometry and Measures • Grade 4–6

Using ruler and compasses, show the region, R, that is

- closer to A than to B
- less than 3 cm from C.

Show your construction lines. (3)

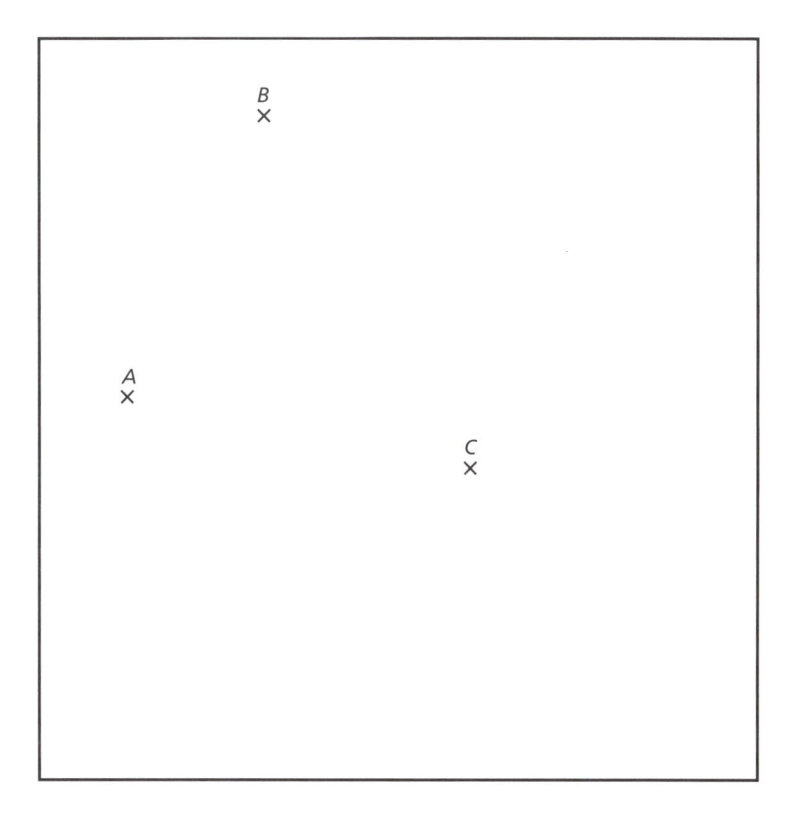

2 Geometry and Measures • Grade 4–6

Using ruler and compasses, construct a net for this tetrahedron (triangular-based pyramid).

Use a scale of 4 cm = 1 cm (3)

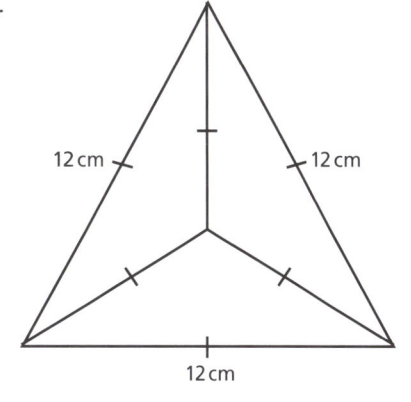

3 Geometry and Measures • Grade 4–6

The diagram shows a rectangle.

Construct the locus of points, outside the rectangle, that are all 2 cm from the edge of the rectangle. **(2)**

4 Geometry and Measures • Grade 4–6

ABC represents a triangular field.

A mobile phone mast is to be built in the field.
The mast will be the same distance from AB as from AC.

Use ruler and compasses to show where the mast could be built.
Show your construction lines. **(3)**

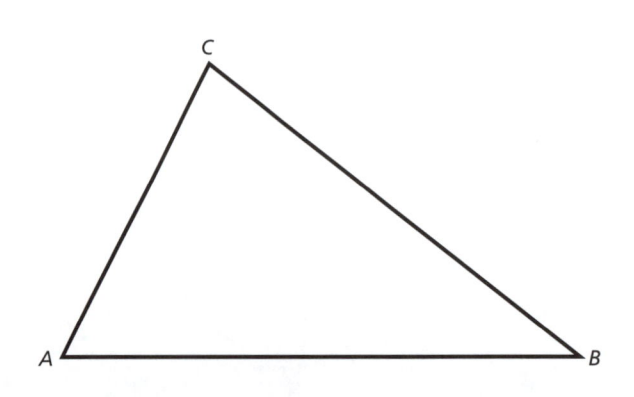

5 Geometry and Measures • Grade 4–6

Here is a plan of a rectangular garden 20 m by 10 m.

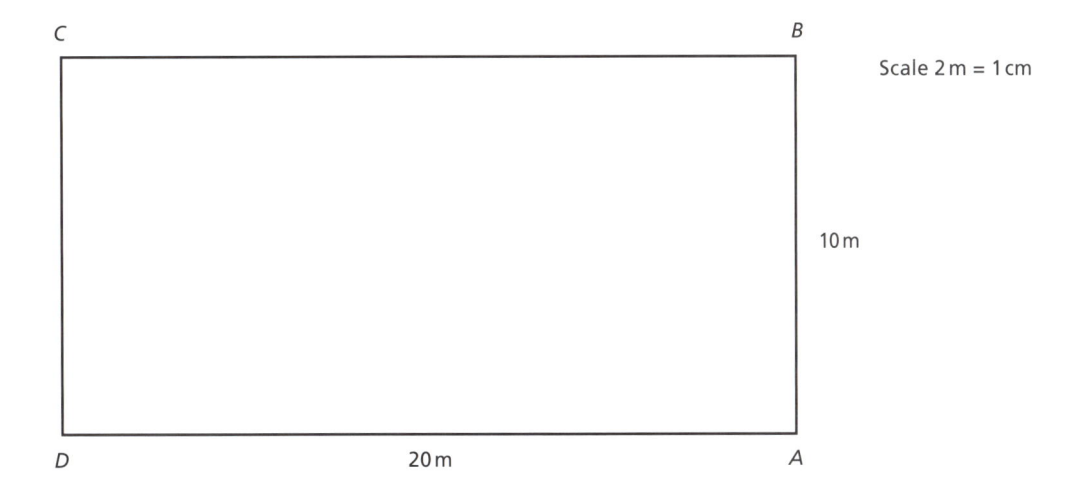

C   B
                                                    Scale 2 m = 1 cm

                                                    10 m

D   20 m   A

Shay wants to plant a tree in the garden.
It must be

- At least 2 m from *AD*
- between 5 m and 10 m from *C*.

Show the region, *R*, where the tree can be planted.
Use a scale of 2 m = 1 cm
Show your construction lines. (3)

Total score: _____ / 14

Give your answer

Write the answer in a particular format, e.g. as a fraction, as a decimal, to a number of decimal places, in terms of π, in a particular unit.

Worked examples and more!

TOP TIP
Make sure you read the whole question. In exam conditions, it is easy to overlook the 'Give your answer...' instruction.

Example questions

1 Number • Grade 4–6

There are 29.2 million males in a country. This is 49% of the population.

Work out the number of females in the country.
Give your answer in standard form. (2)

2 Number • Grade 7–9

Change $0.3\dot{7}$ to a fraction.
Give your answer in its simplest form. (2)

Complete the example

Ratio, Proportion and Rates of Change • Grade 4–6

The volume of a gold bar is 642.5 cm³
The density of gold is 19.3 grams/cm³

Work out the mass of the gold bar.
Give your answer in kilograms to 1 decimal place. (2)

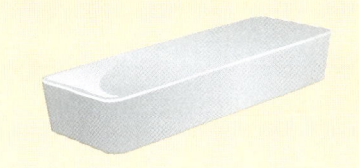

Mass = Volume × Density
Mass = 642.5 × 19.3
Mass = ... grams
Mass = ... kg (to 1 d.p.)

Remember:
Mass / (Volume | Density)

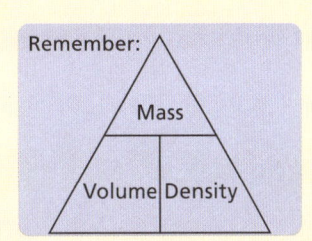

Exam practice questions

1 Number • Grade 4–6

Write 72 as a product of prime factors.
Give your answer in index form. (2)

$2^3 \times 3^2$

2 Number • Grade 4–6

Work out $4\frac{3}{5} \div 1\frac{1}{2}$

Give your answer as a mixed number.

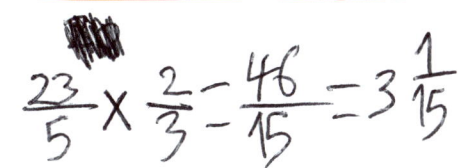

$\frac{23}{5} \times \frac{2}{3} = \frac{46}{15} = 3\frac{1}{15}$

(3)

$3\frac{1}{15}$

3 Number / Algebra • Grade 4–6

a) Simplify $\frac{3^4 \times 3^7}{3^9}$

Give your answer as an integer.

$\frac{3^{11}}{3^9} = 3^2$

(2)

9

b) Simplify $\frac{(7^2)^4}{7^3}$

Give your answer as a power of 7

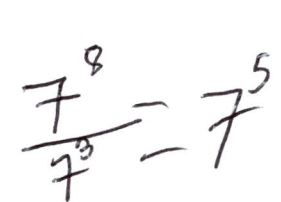

$\frac{7^8}{7^3} = 7^5$

(2)

7^5

4 Ratio, Proportion and Rates of Change / Statistics • Grade 4–6

Here are the masses of four parcels.

    1.5 kg   400 grams   0.75 kg   1 kilogram 200 grams

Work out the median mass.
Give your answer in grams. (2)

.... grams

5 Probability • Grade 7–9

Here are eight cards labelled **X** or **Y**.

Two cards are chosen at random.

    X X X X X X Y Y

Work out the probability that both cards are **X**.
Give your answer as a fraction in its simplest form. (2)

6 Algebra • Grade 7–9

Expand and simplify $(\sqrt{3} + \sqrt{6})^2$
Give your answer in the form $a + b\sqrt{2}$ (3)

7 Algebra • Grade 7–9

Find an approximate solution to $x^2 - 6x - 4 = 0$

Use the iteration $x_{n+1} = \dfrac{4}{x_n - 6}$

Start with $x_1 = 1$
Give your answer to 3 significant figures. (4)

8 Geometry and Measures • Grade 7–9

In the triangle ABC, R is the midpoint of AC.

BS : SC = 3 : 2

$\vec{AB}$ = **a** and $\vec{AC}$ = 2**b**

Work out $\vec{SR}$ in terms of **a** and **b**.
Give your answer in its simplest form. (4)

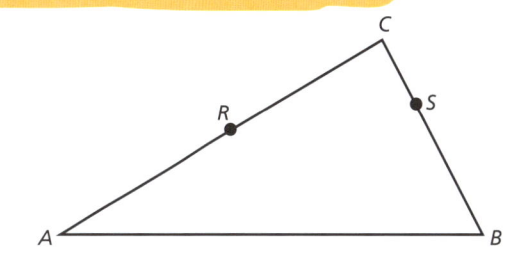

$\vec{SR}$ = ...

9 Geometry and Measures • Grade 7–9

Here is a triangle, ABC.

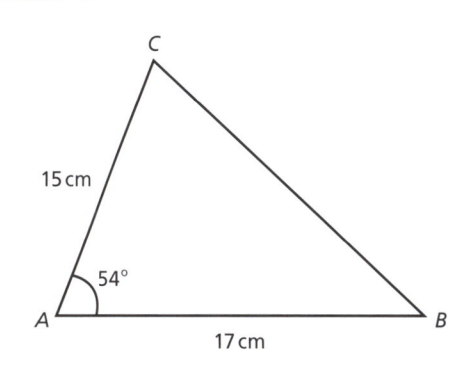

Calculate the length BC.
Give your answer to a suitable degree of accuracy. (3)

BC = *14.64* cm

10 Algebra • Grade 7–9

Solve the quadratic equation $2x^2 - 5x - 6 = 0$
Give your answers to 2 decimal places. (3)

x = ... or x = ...

Total score: .... / 30

Give a reason

Show a calculation, written evidence or an explanation to support your answer or a given statement.

Worked example and more!

TOP TIP
These questions test the depth of your knowledge so make sure you work on any topics you feel less confident about.

Example question

1 Geometry and Measures • Grade 7–9

The diagram shows a right-angled triangle inside a semicircle, centre O.
The triangle ABO is reflected in AB to form a new triangle, ABC.

Will the position of C be on the diameter or outside the semicircle?
Give a reason for your answer.

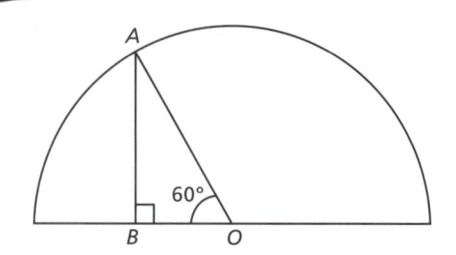

(1)

Complete the example

Geometry and Measures • Grade 4–6

Give a reason why this shape is a trapezium. (1)

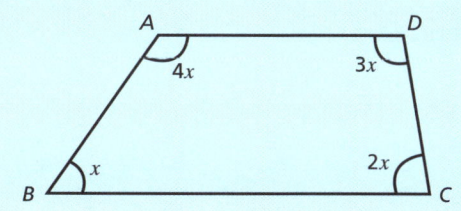

To be a trapezium, one pair of opposite sides would be parallel. The angles in any quadrilateral add up to 360°, so $x + 2x + 3x + 4x = 360°$, giving $10x = 360°$.

Angle A + Angle B = 5x and Angle C + Angle D = ...

This means that Angle A + Angle B = 180° and Angle C + Angle D = ... °

So AD is parallel to ...., meaning that shape ABCD is a trapezium.

Angles inside parallel lines are called allied or co-interior angles.

Exam practice questions

1 Number • Grade 4–6

a) Give a reason why a square number can **never** be prime. (1)

b) Give a reason why the square of an ordinary number cannot be negative. (1)

2 Algebra • Grade 4–6

The nth term of a linear sequence is $6n - 1$

The nth term of a geometric sequence is 2^n

Give a reason why **no** terms appear in both sequences. (1)

3 Number • Grade 4–6

$A = 2^2 \times 3 \times 5^2 \times 7$

$B = 2^3 \times 3 \times 5^2$

Give a reason why the lowest common multiple (LCM) of A and B is **not** $2^2 \times 3 \times 5^2$

Give the actual LCM of A and B. (2)

4 Geometry and Measures • Grade 4–6

Triangle A can be mapped to triangle B using a **single** transformation.

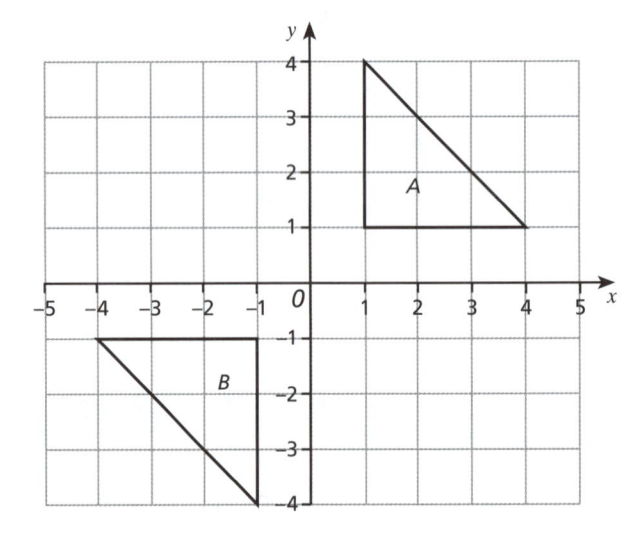

Ekou says, "There is more than one single transformation to map from A to B."

Is he correct?

Give a reason for your answer. (2)

Yes

Reflection in the line $y = -x$

Rotation 180° about the origin

5 Ratio, Proportion and Rates of Change • Grade 4–6

Rentbikes and Cyclesafely hire out scooters.

The graph shows the hire charges for a scooter from Rentbikes.

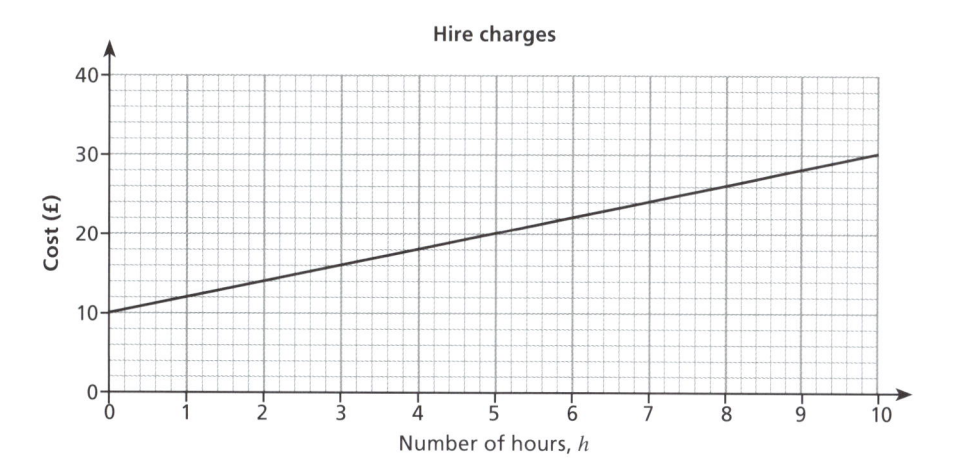

a) Give a reason why the graph starts at £10 (1)

....

b) Cyclesafely charges £4 per hour to hire a scooter.

Is this always cheaper than using Rentbikes?
Give a reason for your answer. (1)

....

....

6 Geometry and Measures • Grade 4–6

A student is asked to calculate the size of angle x by using trigonometry.
He measures the lengths of AB and BC.

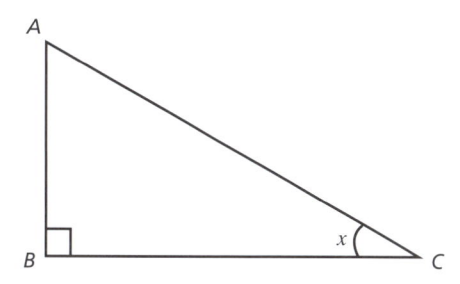

When measured to the nearest centimetre, $AB = 10$ cm and $BC = 15$ cm
When measured to 1 decimal place, $AB = 10.3$ cm and $BC = 15.2$ cm

Which measurements will give the most accurate answer for the size of angle x?
Give a reason for your answer. (1)

....

....

7 Geometry and Measures • Grade 7–9

The diagram shows a circle, centre O, with a straight line ATB touching the circle at T.

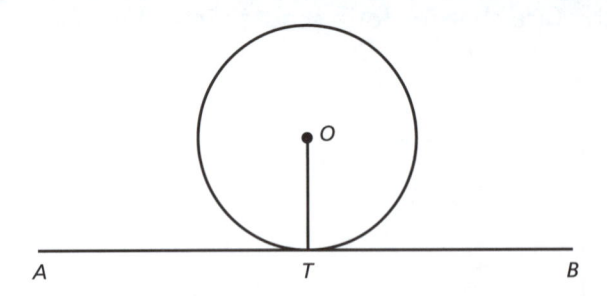

Give a reason why angle OTA is a right angle. (1)

....

....

8 Ratio, Proportion and Rates of Change • Grade 7–9

Here are three statements about shapes A and B.

The volumes are in the ratio 1 : 2
The volumes are in the ratio 1 : 4
The volumes are in the ratio 1 : 8

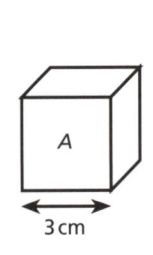

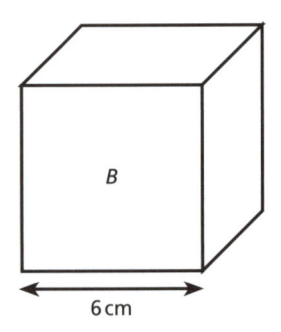

Which statement is correct?
Give a reason for your answer. (1)

....

....

9 Algebra • Grade 7–9

Rufus wants to estimate the area under the curve.
This is his working.

Estimate = $\frac{1}{2} \times 9 \times 4 = 18$ square units

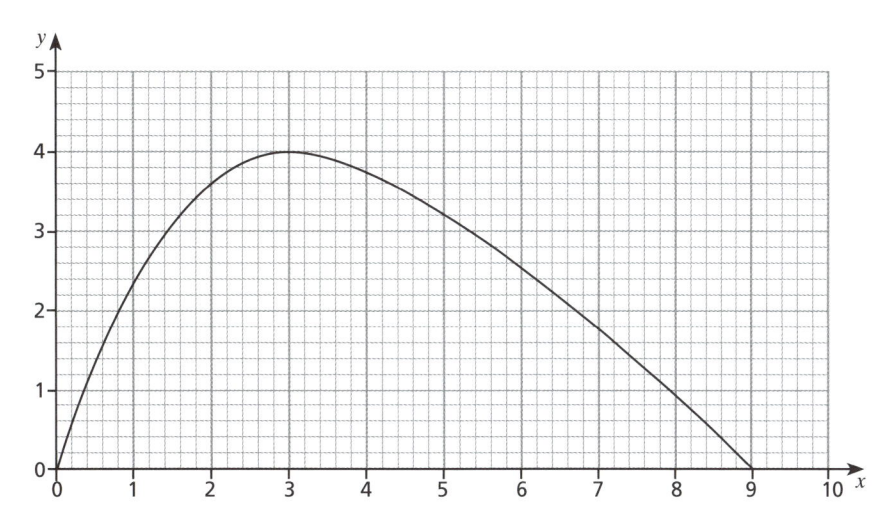

Is his estimate an overestimate or an underestimate?
Give a reason for your answer. (1)

....

....

10 Geometry and Measures • Grade 7–9

The diagram shows a circle, centre O.
ABCD is a cyclic quadrilateral.

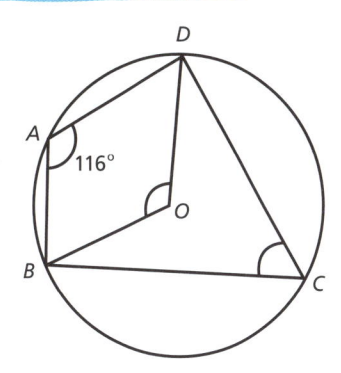

a) Work out the size of angle BCD.
   Give a reason for your answer. (2)

....

....

b) Work out the size of angle BOD.
   Give a reason for your answer. (2)

....

....

Total score: .... / 17

Explain/Justify

Worked example and more!

Explain: Write a sentence or a mathematical statement showing how you got your answer.

Justify: You must show all your working and/or write an explanation.

TOP TIP
Write down every step in your working to support your explanation.

Example question

1 Geometry and Measures • Grade 7–9

T, S and R are points on the circle.
ATB is a tangent to the circle.
The line SR is extended to P.

Work out the size of angle x.

A student writes,
    Angle ATR = 75°
    Angle TRS = 40°
    Angle RTS = 180° − 75° − 40°
             = 65°
    x = 180° − 75° − 65°   Angles on a straight line add up to 180°
    x = 40°

Another student writes,   Angle TRS = 40°
                              So x = 40°

Explain why each student is correct.   (2)

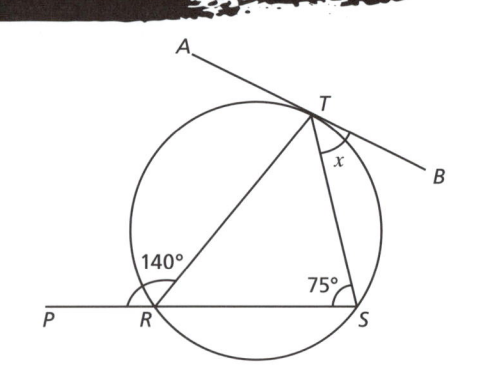

Complete the example

Probability • Grade 4–6

Raj rolls an ordinary dice twice and writes,
The probability of getting a score of 11 $P(11) = P(5) \times P(6)$
$$= \frac{1}{6} \times \frac{1}{6} = \frac{1}{36}$$

Justify why Raj is incorrect. (1)

There are two ways of getting a score of 11. These are 5 and 6 or 6 and 5. Raj has only worked out the probability of one way.

The probability of getting a score of 11 $P(11) = P(5) \times P(6) \times 2$

$$= \frac{}{} \times \frac{}{} \times \underline{} = \frac{}{}$$

Exam practice questions

1 Number • Grade 4–6

Mia is trying to convert numbers into standard form.

a) She writes, $1\,230\,000 = 123 \times 10^4$

Explain the mistake she has made. (1)

b) She then writes, $0.004\,56 = 4.56 \times 10^3$

Explain the mistake she has made. (1)

2 Statistics • Grade 4–6

The table shows information about the weekly earnings of 60 employees.

Weekly earnings (£x)	Frequency
$400 < x \leq 500$	3
$500 < x \leq 600$	27
$600 < x \leq 700$	15
$700 < x \leq 800$	9
$800 < x \leq 900$	6

The mean of the weekly earnings is £630

Yuri says,   "The mean may not be the best average to use to represent this information."

Do you agree with Yuri?
You **must** justify your answer. (1)

3 Statistics • Grade 4–6

The scatter graph shows information about the value and ages of some cars.
Benji has drawn a line of best fit onto the scatter graph.

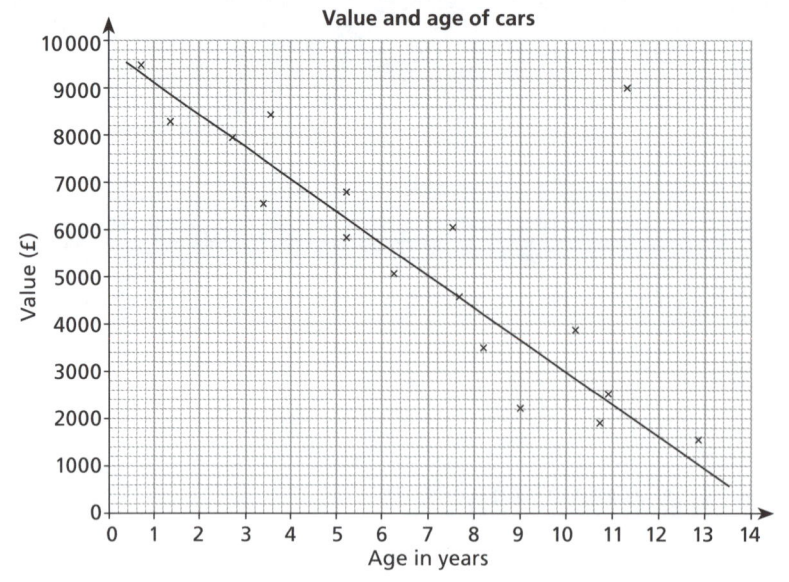

Benji says there is no correlation between the ages and values of the cars because the points don't all follow the line of best fit.

Explain why Benji is wrong. (1)

....

....

4 Ratio, Proportion and Rates of Change • Grade 4–6

There are some blue buttons and some green buttons in a bag.
The buttons are either round or square.

The ratio of blue buttons to green buttons is 3 : 7
The ratio of round buttons to square buttons is 5 : 2

Explain why the least possible number of buttons in the bag is 70 (1)

....

....

5 Statistics • Grade 7–9

An office manager draws this histogram to show the times taken to complete a job.

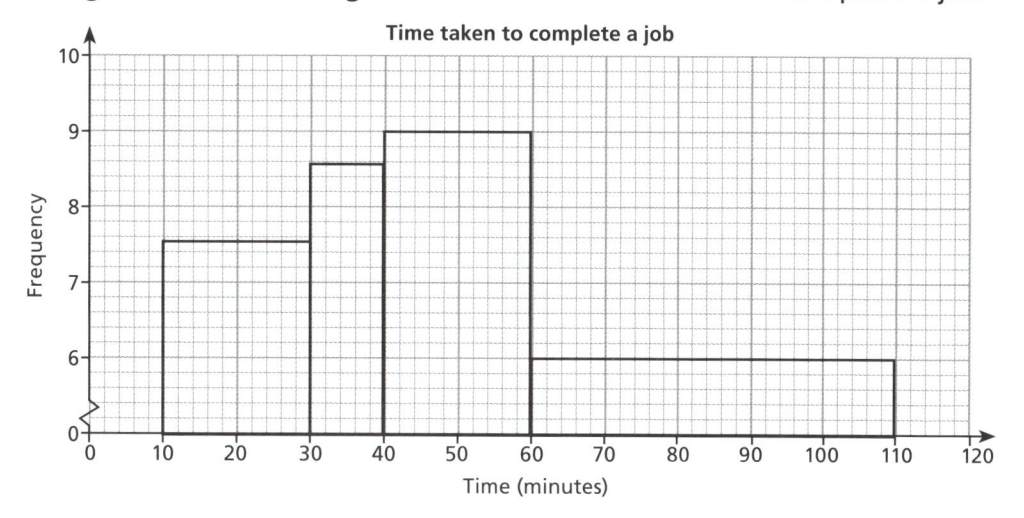

Time taken to complete a job

Explain **two** errors they have made with the histogram. (2)

6 Number • Grade 7–9

Julia has to work out the exact value of $27^{-\frac{1}{3}}$

Julia says, $\frac{1}{3}$ of 27 is 9   so $27^{-\frac{1}{3}} = -9$

Explain the **two** mistakes Julia has made. (2)

Total score: / 9

Prove that/Show (that)

Give a formal algebraic proof or a formal geometric proof. Each step needs to be shown, with reasons where required. Write your workings to clarify how you chose an answer so it is clear that you are not guessing.

Worked example and more!

TOP TIP
Show the methods that you are using to prove the statement.

Example question

1 Geometry and Measures • Grade 7–9

ABCD is a cyclic quadrilateral as shown.
AD = BD

Prove that $y = 90° + x$

(4)

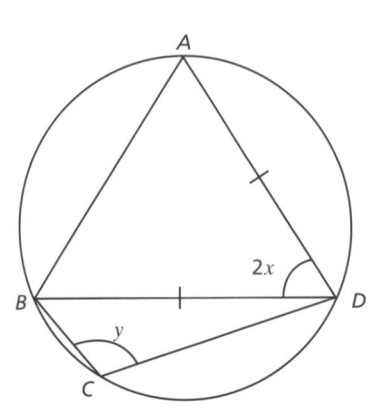

Complete the example

Algebra • Grade 7–9

Prove that the square of any odd number is always odd.

> The question is asking you to prove that (odd number)² = odd number

Let x be any integer.

So any odd numbers would be of the form $2x + 1$

(odd number)² can be written as $(2x + 1)^2$

Expanding the expression $\quad (2x + 1)(2x + 1) = 4x^2 + 2x + \underline{} + \underline{}$

Simplifying $\quad\quad\quad\quad\quad\quad\quad\quad\quad = 4x^2 + \underline{} + \underline{}$

$\quad\quad\quad\quad\quad\quad\quad\quad\quad\quad\quad\quad = 4(x^2 + x) + \underline{}$

$4(x^2 + x)$ must be even as any multiple of 4 is even.

So $4(x^2 + x) + \underline{}$ is always $\underline{}$.

Exam practice questions

⏱ 42

1 Geometry and Measures • Grade 4–6

The diagram shows a trapezium.

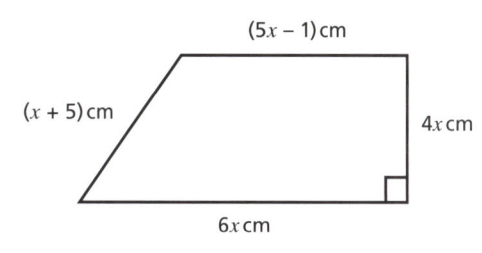

Top: $(5x - 1)$ cm
Left slant: $(x + 5)$ cm
Right: $4x$ cm
Bottom: $6x$ cm

a) Show that the perimeter is $(16x + 4)$ cm (1)

b) If $x = 1.5$, show that two of the sides have the same length. (2)

2 Ratio, Proportion and Rates of Change • Grade 4–6

On the number line, the ratio $x : y = 5 : 2$

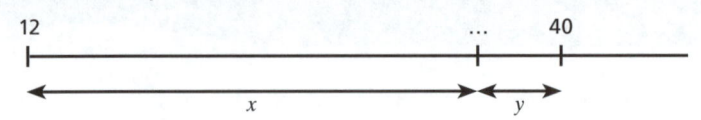

Show that the missing value is 32 (3)

3 Algebra / Geometry and Measures • Grade 4–6

The diagram shows a parallelogram.
The perimeter is 28 cm.

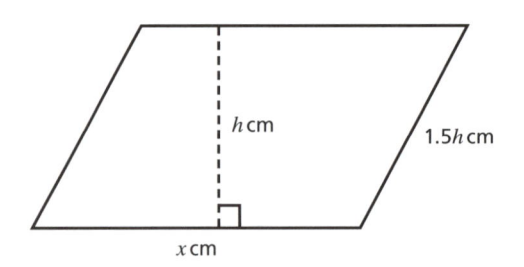

a) Show that $2x + 3h = 28$ (1)

b) Show that if $x = 8$ cm, the area of the parallelogram is 32 cm² (3)

4 Algebra • Grade 4–6

n is a positive integer.

Show that $(n + 1)^2 + (n - 1)^2$ is always even. (3)

108

5 Geometry and Measures • Grade 4–6

The diagram shows an isosceles triangle ABD.

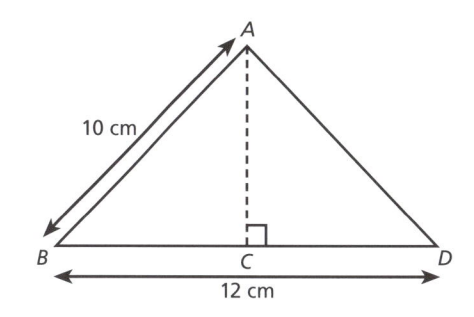

AB = 10 cm
BD = 12 cm

Show that the area of triangle ABD = 48 cm² (4)

6 Ratio, Proportion and Rates of Change • Grade 7–9

You are given that   Surface area of a sphere = $4\pi r^2$

Two spheres have diameters in the ratio   2 : 7

Show that the ratio of the surface areas is   1 : 12.25 (2)

7 Geometry and Measures • Grade 7–9

a) Show that   2sin 45°cos 45° = sin 90° (2)

b) Show that   2sin 30°cos 30° = sin 60° (3)

8 Algebra • Grade 7–9

n is a positive integer.

Prove that $(4n + 3)^2 - (4n - 3)^2$ is a multiple of 8 (3)

9 Algebra • Grade 7–9

The graphs of $y = x^2 + 6$ and $y + 4x = 30$ are shown on the grid.

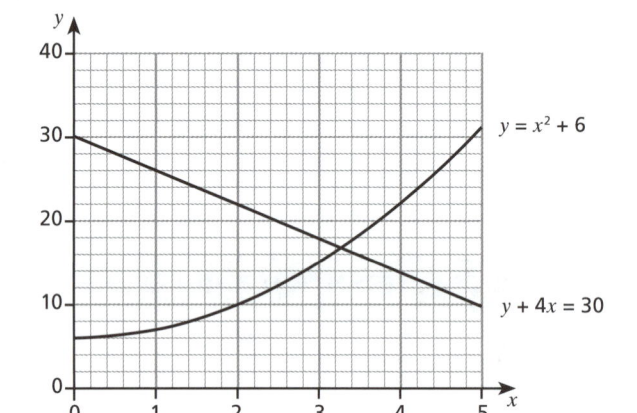

Show clearly that the intersection of the graphs will give a solution to the equation
$x^2 + 4x - 24 = 0$ (2)

10 Probability • Grade 7–9

A bag contains 20 counters. They are either red counters or green counters.
Three counters are taken from the bag at random.

The probability that the three counters taken are all red is $\frac{1}{114}$

Show that there are 15 green counters in the bag. (2)

11 Number • Grade 7–9

Show that $(\sqrt{2} + \sqrt{6})^2 - (2 + \sqrt{3})^2 = 1$ (3)

12 Algebra • Grade 7–9

$u_{n+1} = 6u_n - 5$ and $u_1 = 2$

a) Show that $u_2 = 7$ (1)

b) Show that $u_{n+2} = 36u_n - 35$ (2)

13 Geometry and Measures • Grade 7–9

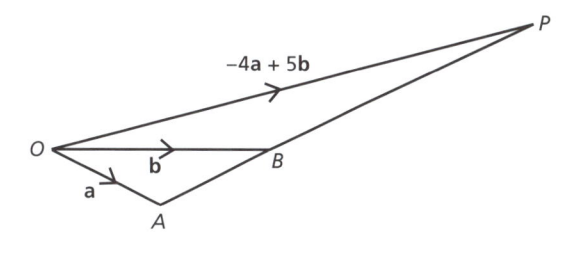

$\vec{OA} = \mathbf{a}$
$\vec{OB} = \mathbf{b}$
$\vec{OP} = -4\mathbf{a} + 5\mathbf{b}$

Prove that ABP is a straight line. (3)

Total score: / 40

Mixed Questions

1 Algebra • Grade 4–6

a) Given that $n = 4$, which of these expressions have the same value? (3)

n^2 16	$2n^2$ 32	2^n 16
$4n$ 16	$16n^0$ 16	$16n$ 64

$n^2, 2^n, 4n, 16n^0$

b) Given that n is odd, show that **two** of these expressions are odd. (3)

n^2	$(n + 1)^2$	$(n - 1)^2$
$1 + n^2$	$n^2 - 1$	$2 + n^2$

2 Ratio, Proportion and Rates of Change • Grade 4–6

a) The total cost of three dresses in a shop is £120
All prices increase by 5%.

Work out the mean cost of a dress after the increase. (3)

£ ....

b) A shirt that is normally £28 is on sale with 10% off.
Trousers that are normally £42 are on sale with 20% off.

Leo says that the trousers now cost less than the shirt because 20% is greater than 10%.

Is he correct?
Show working to support your answer. (3)

3 Probability • Grade 4–6

Here is a Venn diagram.

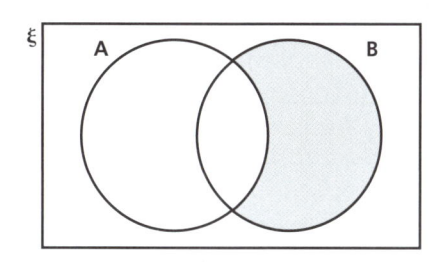

a) Describe the shaded region using set notation. (1)

B'

b) Describe in words what A ∩ B represents. (1)

4 Number / Probability • Grade 4–6

100 people take two tests, A and B.
54 pass test A.
28 pass both tests.
Half of the people who failed test A also failed test B.

a) Complete the frequency tree. (3)

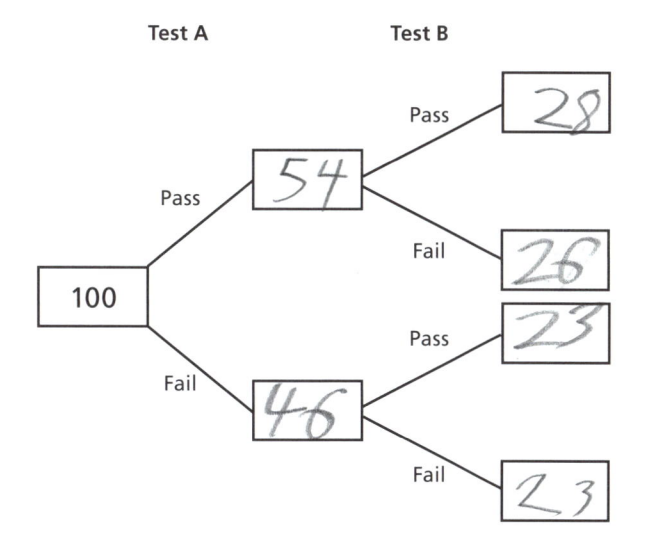

- 100
  - Pass: 54
    - Pass: 28
    - Fail: 26
  - Fail: 46
    - Pass: 23
    - Fail: 23

b) How many more people passed test A than passed test B? (1)

28

5 Number / Ratio, Proportion and Rates of Change • Grade 4–6

A student wants to colour in some of the small squares in this grid.

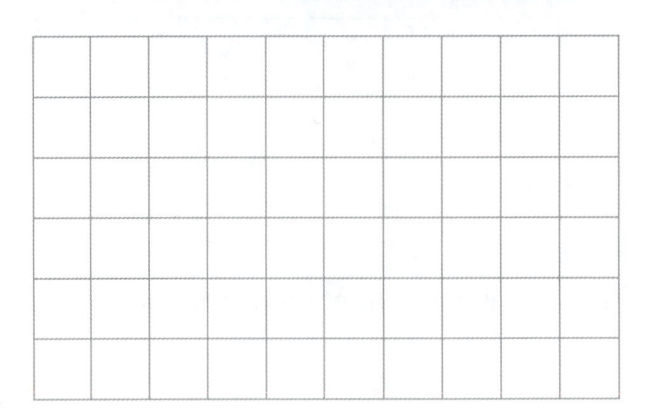

30% of the squares are coloured grey.
50% of remaining squares are coloured red.

a) What percentage of the squares are **not** coloured? (3)

.... %

b) One-half of the grey squares and two-thirds of the red squares are on an outside edge.

What proportion of **all** the squares are coloured and **not** on an outside edge?
Give your answer as a fraction in its simplest form. (2)

....

6 Algebra • Grade 4–6

Match each graph to its equation by writing the correct letter in the table.

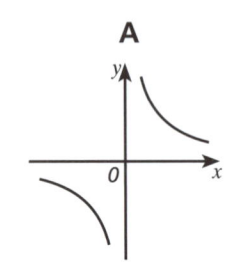

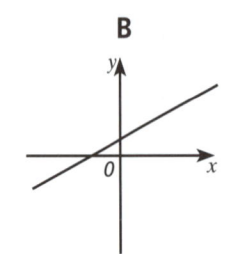

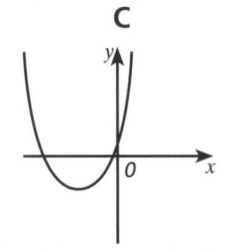

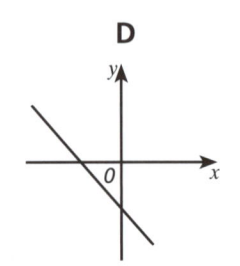

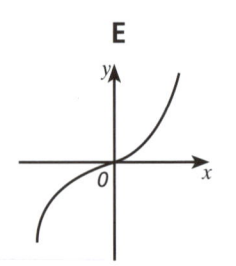

A   B   C   D   E

Equation	Graph
$y = x^2 + 3x + 2$	
$y = 2x^3$	
$y = -2x - 3$	
$y = \frac{3}{x}$	
$y = x + 3$	

(3)

7 Statistics • Grade 4–6

The stem and leaf diagram shows information about the lengths, in centimetres, of 15 pieces of ribbon.

11	2 7
12	1 3 4 6 9
13	2 3 3 4 7 9
14	4 7

Key: 11|2 represents 112 cm

On the grid, draw a box plot for this information.

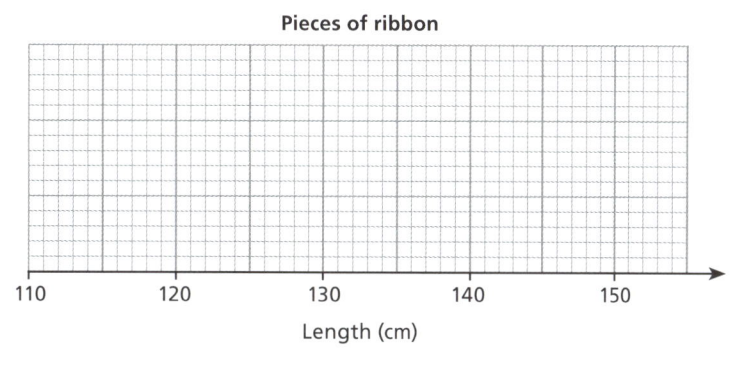

Pieces of ribbon

Length (cm)

(3)

8 Statistics • Grade 4–6

The table gives information about the heights, in centimetres, of some plants.

Height (h cm)	Frequency
$0 < h \leq 20$	5
$20 < h \leq 40$	20
$40 < h \leq 60$	60
$60 < h \leq 80$	35
$80 < h \leq 100$	15

Leona draws a frequency polygon for the information in the table.

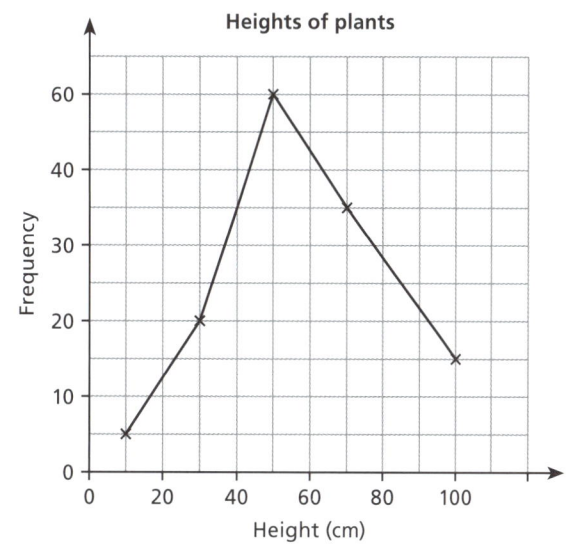

Heights of plants

Write down **two** mistakes Leona has made. (2)

....

....

9 Number • Grade 7–9

a) Simplify fully $(2\sqrt{3})^2$ (1)

b) Write $\dfrac{4}{\sqrt{2}} + \sqrt{32}$ in the form $a\sqrt{2}$ where a is an integer. (3)

10 Ratio, Proportion and Rates of Change / Geometry and Measures • Grade 7–9

The diagram shows a triangle and a circle.

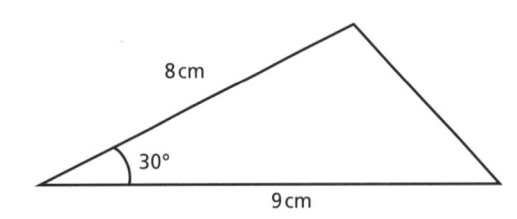

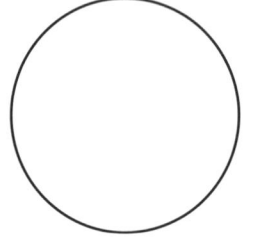

(triangle with sides 8 cm and 9 cm, included angle 30°; circle)

a) Work out the area of the triangle. (2)

.... cm²

b) The ratio area of triangle to area of circle = 2 : 3

Calculate the radius of the circle.
Give your answer to 1 decimal place. (3)

.... cm

11 Algebra • Grade 7–9

a) Show that $\dfrac{1}{x+1} - \dfrac{1}{x-4} = 3$ simplifies to $3x^2 - 9x - 7 = 0$ (4)

b) Hence, solve $\dfrac{1}{x+1} - \dfrac{1}{x-4} = 3$

Give your answers to 2 decimal places. (3)

$x =$ .... or $x =$ ....

12 Geometry and Measures • Grade 7–9

The diagram shows a quadrilateral PQRS.

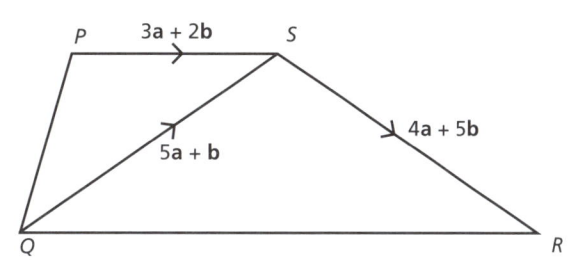

P —— 3a + 2b —— S, with 5a + b from Q to S, and 4a + 5b from S to R.

a) Work out QR in terms of **a** and **b**. (1)

b) What type of quadrilateral is PQRS?
Give a reason for your answer. (1)

13 Probability • Grade 7–9

In the Venn diagram

ξ = number of people in a shopping centre during lunchtime
A = number of people who visit a snack bar
B = number of people who visit a café

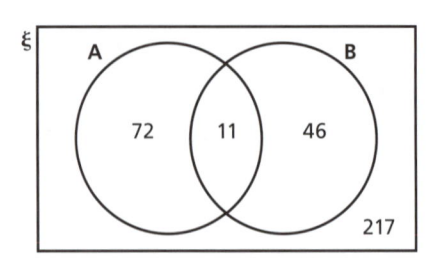

[Venn diagram: A contains 72, intersection 11, B contains 46, outside 217]

a) How many of these people visited the snack bar, the café or both? (1)

b) One person is chosen at random.

Work out the probability that the person visited the snack bar. (1)

c) One person who visited the café is chosen at random.

Work out the probability that the person also visited the snack bar. (1)

14 Statistics • Grade 7–9

Ali wants to estimate the number of frogs in a pond.

On Saturday, Ali catches 24 frogs from the pond.
He puts a tag on each of the frogs and puts them back into the pond.

On Sunday, Ali catches 40 frogs from the same pond.
He finds that 6 of the 40 frogs are tagged.

Work out an estimate for the total number of frogs in the pond. (3)

15 Geometry and Measures • Grade 7–9

The diagram shows an ellipse.

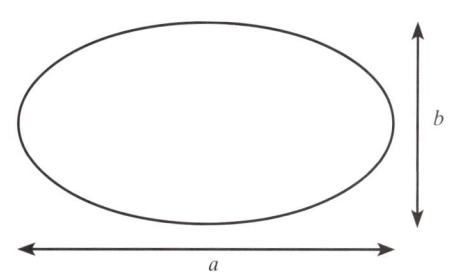

The formula for the area of an ellipse, with width a and height b, is   Area = $\frac{\pi ab}{4}$

This diagram shows a circle with an ellipse removed.

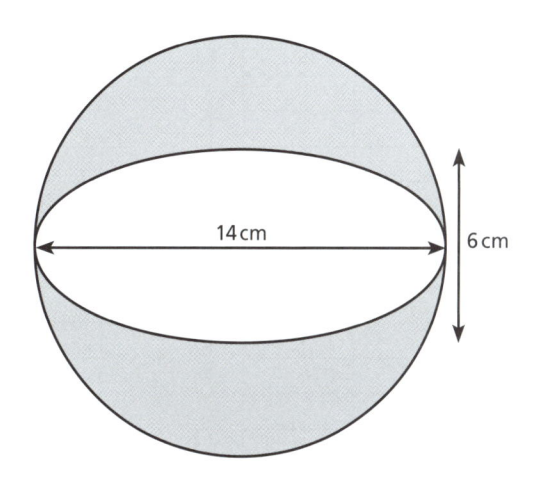

Work out the shaded area.
Give your answer in terms of π. (3)

.... cm²

16 Algebra • Grade 7–9

Rhys expands the brackets $(3m + 2)(m - 5)(2m + 7)$

He writes, $(3m + 2)(m - 5)(2m + 7)$

$= (3m^2 - 15m + 2m - 10)(2m + 7)$

$= (3m^2 - 13m - 10)(2m + 7)$

$= 6m^3 + 21m^2 - 26m^2 - 91m - 20m + 70$

$= 6m^3 - 5m^2 - 71m + 70$

Explain the mistakes he has made. (2)

Total score: .... / 60

Index of Topics

This index tells you which questions in this book offer practice for each of the six specification topics.

Topic	Page	Question	Example question	Complete the example	Exam practice question
Number	5	1			✓
	6	7			✓
	8	1	✓		
	10	3			✓
	11	6			✓
	11	7			✓
	14	1	✓		
	17	4			✓
	21			✓	
	21	1			✓
	27			✓	
	28	4			✓
	30	1	✓		
	31			✓	
	31	1			✓
	31	2			✓
	31	4			✓
	32	2	✓		
	35	8			✓
	35	9			✓
	37			✓	
	39	8			✓
	39	10			✓
	53	1			✓
	56	1	✓		
	68	3			✓
	69	5			✓
	72	3			✓
	92	1	✓		
	92	2	✓		
	93	1			✓
	93	2			✓
	93	3			✓
	97	1			✓
	98	3			✓
	103	1			✓
	105	6			✓
	111	11			✓
	113	4			✓
	114	5			✓
	116	9			✓
Algebra	4	1	✓		
	5			✓	
	6	5			✓
	7	9			✓

Topic	Page	Question	Example question	Complete the example	Exam practice question
Algebra (cont.)	7	10			✓
	10	4			✓
	12	10			✓
	13	11			✓
	14	2	✓		
	18	7			✓
	20	2	✓		
	22	2			✓
	24	8			✓
	24	9			✓
	25	10			✓
	25	11			✓
	27			✓	
	27	2			✓
	29	6			✓
	30	2	✓		
	32	1	✓		
	33			✓	
	33	1			✓
	33	2			✓
	34	3			✓
	35	6			✓
	35	7			✓
	36	1	✓		
	36	2	✓		
	37	1			✓
	37	2			✓
	38	3			✓
	38	4			✓
	38	5			✓
	38	6			✓
	38	7			✓
	39	9			✓
	40	1	✓		
	40	2	✓		
	41			✓	
	41	1			✓
	42	2			✓
	42	3			✓
	43	4			✓
	43	5			✓
	43	6			✓
	43	7			✓
	44	1	✓		

Topic	Page	Question	Example question	Complete the example	Exam practice question
Algebra (cont.)	44	2	✓		
	45			✓	
	45	1			✓
	45	2			✓
	45	3			✓
	46	4			✓
	46	5			✓
	46	6			✓
	46	7			✓
	47	8			✓
	47	9			✓
	47	10			✓
	49			✓	
	50	1			✓
	51	3			✓
	51	4			✓
	55	5			✓
	55	7			✓
	60	1	✓		
	60	2	✓		
	63	4			✓
	65	7			✓
	65	8			✓
	69	7			✓
	72	2			✓
	75	8			✓
	75	9			✓
	80	1	✓		
	82	1			✓
	83	3			✓
	83	4			✓
	84	6			✓
	85	7			✓
	93	3			✓
	94	6			✓
	94	7			✓
	95	10			✓
	97	2			✓
	101	9			✓
	107			✓	
	108	3			✓
	108	4			✓
	110	8			✓
	110	9			✓
	111	12			✓
	112	1			✓
	114	6			✓
	117	11			✓
	119	16			✓
Ratio, Proportion and Rates of Change	7	11			✓
	9	1			✓
	11	5			✓
	12	8			✓
	15	1			✓
Ratio, Proportion and Rates of Change (cont.)	16	2			✓
	16	3			✓
	20	1	✓		
	23	4			✓
	27	1			✓
	31	3			✓
	53	2			✓
	59	5			✓
	63	3			✓
	68	2			✓
	71			✓	
	93			✓	
	94	4			✓
	99	5			✓
	100	8			✓
	104	4			✓
	108	2			✓
	109	6			✓
	112	2			✓
	114	5			✓
	116	10			✓
Geometry and Measures	5	2			✓
	6	4			✓
	7	12			✓
	9			✓	
	13	12			✓
	15			✓	
	17	5			✓
	18	6			✓
	19	8			✓
	23	5			✓
	23	6			✓
	24	7			✓
	26	1	✓		
	26	2	✓		✓
	27			✓	
	28	3			✓
	28	5			✓
	29	8			✓
	34	4			✓
	34	5			✓
	35	9			✓
	39	9			✓
	48	1	✓		
	50	2			✓
	58	2			✓
	62	1			✓
	62	2			✓
	66	1	✓		
	67	1			✓
	70	1	✓		
	72	1			✓
	74	7			✓

Topic	Page	Question	Example question	Complete the example	Exam practice question	Topic	Page	Question	Example question	Complete the example	Exam practice question
Geometry and Measures (cont.)	76	1	✓			Probability (cont.)	12	9			✓
	77			✓			22	3			✓
	78	1			✓		29	7			✓
	78	2			✓		52	1	✓		
	79	3			✓		58	3			✓
	79	4			✓		69	6			✓
	81			✓			73	5			✓
	82	2			✓		94	5			✓
	83	3			✓		103			✓	
	86	1	✓				110	10			✓
	86	2	✓				113	3			✓
	87			✓			113	4			✓
	89	1			✓		118	13			✓
	89	2			✓	Statistics	6	8			✓
	90	3			✓		11	6			✓
	90	4			✓		19	9			✓
	91	5			✓		33	1			✓
	95	8			✓		53			✓	
	95	9			✓		54	3			✓
	96	1	✓				54	4			✓
	97			✓			55	6			✓
	98	4			✓		57			✓	
	99	6			✓		58	1			✓
	100	7			✓		59	4			✓
	101	10			✓		61			✓	
	102	1	✓				64	5			✓
	106	1	✓				64	6			✓
	107	1			✓		67			✓	
	108	3			✓		68	4			✓
	109	5			✓		73	4			✓
	109	7			✓		74	6			✓
	111	13			✓		83	5			✓
	116	10			✓		94	4			✓
	117	12			✓		103	2			✓
	119	15			✓		104	3			✓
Probability	5	3			✓		105	5			✓
	6	6			✓		115	7			✓
	8	2	✓				115	8			✓
	10	2			✓		118	14			✓

Answers

Pages 4–7: Write (down)
Complete the example
Completing the square gives $x^2 - 8x = (x-4)^2 - 16$
So $\quad x^2 - 8x + 15 = (x-4)^2 - 16 + \mathbf{15}$
$\quad\quad x^2 - 8x + 15 = (x-4)^2 - \mathbf{1}$

Exam practice questions
1. $42 = 2 \times 3 \times 7$ [1]
   $6804 = 2 \times 3^4 \times 2 \times 3 \times 7 = 2^2 \times 3^5 \times 7$ [1]
2. a) $\sin x = \frac{2}{9}$ [1]
   b) 1.5 or $\frac{3}{2}$ [1]
   c) $y = 9 \times 1.5$ or $9 + 4.5 = 13.5$ [1]
3. $\frac{1}{3} \times \frac{1}{3} = \frac{1}{9}$ [1]
4. 20° and 140° [1]
   or 80° and 80° [1]
5. $3n - 1$ [2]
   [1 mark for $3n + c$]
6. It does not land on heads $80 - 47 = 33$ times, so relative frequency that it does not land on heads $= \frac{33}{80}$ [1]
7. 3 600 000 [1]
8. a) 42 [1]
   b) $90 - 10 = 80$ [1]
   c) $80 - 26 = 54$ [1]
9. $a = -2$ **[1]**, $b = 1$ **[1]**, $c = 3$ **[1]**
10. $f^{-1}(x) = \frac{x}{5}$ [1]
11. a) $2^2 : 5^2 = 4 : 25$ [1]
    b) $2^3 : 5^3 = 8 : 125$ [1]
12. a) $(0, 0)$ [1]
    b) 7 units [1]

Pages 8–13: Which / What / When
Complete the example
a) This gives $A = \frac{1}{2} \times \mathbf{11} \times \mathbf{6} \sin x$
   $A = \mathbf{33} \sin x \text{ cm}^2$
b) $A = 33 \sin 30°$
   $A = 33 \times \frac{\mathbf{1}}{\mathbf{2}}$
   $A = \mathbf{16.5} \text{ cm}^2$

Exam practice questions
1. £538.45 [2]
   [1 mark for 500×1.025^n ($n = 1, 2$ or 3)]
2. $\frac{1}{216}$ [2]
   [1 mark for $\left(\frac{1}{6}\right)^3$]
3. a) 9.5 cm [1]
   b) 52 [2]
   [1 mark for $500 \div 9.5$ or $52.6...$]
4. x^3 [1]
5. 13 [3]
   [2 marks for $20 \div 1.5$ or 13.33; 1 mark for 1.5 cups of flour per dough]
6. a) 40 years [2]
   [1 mark for 60 or 20 used]
   b) 20% [2]
   [1 mark for $\frac{30}{150}$ or $\frac{1}{5}$]

7. $50, 100, 150, ...$ and $120, 240, 360$ or $2, 4, 6$ [1]
   600 minutes or 10 hours [1]
   8 pm [1]
8. 17.5% **[3]** decrease **[1]**
   [2 marks for using a suitable example, such as:
   Assume
   In February 40 ovens sold at £100 = £4000
   In March 30 ovens sold at £110 = £3300 [1]
   So decrease = £700 [1]
9. a) $\frac{4}{7}$ [2]
   [1 mark for 4 red and 3 white]
   b) $\frac{5}{14}$ [2]
   [1 mark for $\frac{5}{8} \times \frac{4}{7}$]
10. Equation is of the form $ax^2 + bx + c = 0$
    Quadratic formula is $x = \frac{-b \pm \sqrt{b^2 - 4ac}}{2a}$
    So $2a = 4$, giving $a = 2$
    $-b = 3$, giving $b = -3$
    $4ac = -56$, $8c = -56$, giving $c = -7$
    Quadratic equation is $2x^2 - 3x - 7 = 0$ [3]
    [2 marks for two or three correct coefficients; 1 mark for one correct coefficient]
11. a) 5 seconds [1]
    b) Any answer in the range 3.5 to 4 seconds [1]
12. Volume of hemisphere $\frac{2}{3}\pi(2r)^3 = \frac{16}{3}\pi r^3$ [1]
    Volume of cone $\frac{1}{3}\pi(3r)^2(2r) = 6\pi r^3$ [1]
    Cone has bigger volume [1]

Pages 14–19: How… long / many / much / does
Complete the example
Using the formula $\frac{1}{2}ab\sin C$ to find the area of the garden:
$\frac{1}{2} \times \mathbf{7.9} \times \mathbf{8.6} \times \sin \mathbf{64°} = \mathbf{30.53...} \text{ m}^2$
To find the number of bags of fertiliser needed, divide the area by 3.25
$\mathbf{30.53...} \div 3.25 = \mathbf{9.39...}$
So rounding up, **10** whole bags of fertiliser are needed.

Exam practice questions
1. a) £4817.70 [2]
   [1 mark for 4500×1.023^3]
   b) 31 years [2]
   [1 mark for 4500×1.023^x where $x > 3$]
2. a) £27.12 [4]
   **[1 mark for $189 \div 1.6 \times 0.45$ or 53.16 or 5316;
   1 mark for $189 \div 9 \times 1.24$ or 21×124 or 2604
   or £26.04; 1 mark for '53.16' – '26.04' or 2712]**
   b) Lewis would get **less** money, **or** it would **reduce** [1]
3. 1.5 litres [1]
4. 500 [2]
   [1 mark for $1 \times 10 \times 10 \times 5$ or $\frac{10 \times 10 \times 10}{2}$ or $\frac{1000}{2}$]
5. 15 units [2]
   [1 mark for $\sqrt{((-7-2)^2 + (7-(-5))^2)}$ or $\sqrt{(81 + 144)}$ or $\sqrt{225}$]

6. $(AC)^2 = 7^2 + 9.5^2 - (2 \times 7 \times 9.5 \times \cos 77)$ [1]
   $AC = 10.456...$ km [1]
   Time $= \frac{AC}{4.8} = 2.178...$ hours [1]
   2 hours and 11 minutes [1]

7. a) 3 seconds [1]
   b) 1 m/s [accept 0.8 to 1.2 m/s] [2]
      [1 mark for correct tangent drawn at 2 seconds;
      1 mark for correct gradient of tangent drawn]

8. 180 spheres [6]
   [1 mark for $30 \times 30 \times 7$ or 6300; 1 mark for '6300' $\times$ 15 or 94 500; 1 mark for $\frac{4}{3}\pi 5^3$ or $\frac{500}{3}\pi$ or 523.5... or 524; 1 mark for '94 500' $\div$ '523.5...'; 1 mark for 180.(481...); 1 mark for 180 or correctly rounded number from previous mark]

9. 50 [3]
   [1 mark for 10×1 or 5×2 or 10×1.5 or 15×1; 1 mark for $10 + 10 + 15 + 15$]

Pages 20–25: Work out / Find

Complete the example

So we use the upper bound for b and the lower bound for c.
The upper bound for $b = $ **5.65**
The lower bound for $c = $ **4.025**
This gives the upper bound for $a = \frac{5.65^2}{4.025} = 7.931055901$
$a = $ **7.931** to 3 d.p.

Exam practice questions

1. 2520 or $2^3 \times 3^2 \times 5 \times 7$ [3]
   [1 mark for identifying 2^3; 1 mark for identifying 3^2]

2. $a = -5$ $b = -20$ [3]
   [1 mark for $4ax - 3a$; 1 mark for $a = -5$]

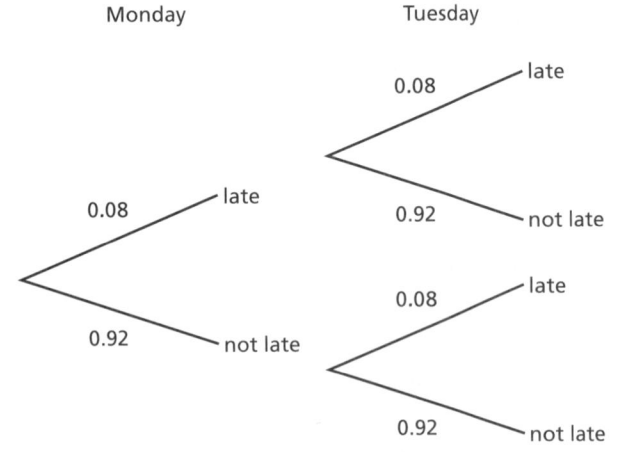

3. 0.1536 [4]

   Monday   Tuesday
                 0.08 — late
         0.08 — late
                 0.92 — not late
                 0.08 — late
         0.92 — not late
                 0.92 — not late

   [1 mark for completed tree diagram with correct values on branches; 1 mark for 0.08×0.92 or 0.92×0.08 (= 0.0736) or 0.08×0.08 (= 0.0064) or 0.92×0.92 (= 0.8464); 1 mark for '0.0064' + 2 $\times$ '0.0736' or 1 – '0.8464']

4. 55% [2]
   [1 mark for $\frac{11}{6 + 11 + 3}$ $(= \frac{11}{20})$]

5. 18° [3]
   [1 mark for finding interior or exterior angle of 10-sided regular polygon $\frac{360°}{10}$ (= 36°) or $\frac{8 \times 180°}{10}$ (= 144°); 1 mark for 36° $\div$ 2 or $\frac{180° - 144°}{2}$]

6. 240 cm² [4]
   [1 mark for finding scale factor $\frac{30}{12}$ or $\frac{5}{2}$ or 2.5, or $\frac{12}{30}$ or $\frac{2}{5}$ or 0.4; 1 mark for 2.5^2 or 6.25 or $\frac{25}{4}$, or 0.4^2 or 0.16 or $\frac{4}{25}$; 1 mark for $1500 \div 2.5^2$ or 6.25 or $\frac{25}{4}$, or 1500×0.4^2 or 0.16 or $\frac{4}{25}$]

7. $7\sqrt{3}$ cm [3]
   [1 mark for $\sin 30° = \frac{1}{2}$ or $\sin 60° = \frac{\sqrt{3}}{2}$ or $\sin 120° = \frac{\sqrt{3}}{2}$ or $\cos 120 = -\frac{1}{2}$; 1 mark for $\frac{7}{\sin 30} = \frac{x}{\sin 120}$ or $14 \times \sin 60° = x$ or $x^2 = 7^2 + 7^2 - (2 \times 7 \times 7 \times \cos 120°)$]

8. $2n^2 - n + 3$ [3]
   [1 mark for $2n^2$ or n^2; 1 mark for $2n^2$ and either $-n$ or $+3$]

9. $x^2 - 8x + 1$ [2]
   [1 mark for $(x - 4)^2 - 15$]

10. 13, 7, 8 [3]
    [1 mark for $(3x + 1)(x + 4)$ or $(3x + 4)(x + 1)$ or $(3x + 2)(x + 2)$; 1 mark for $(3x^2 + 13x + 4)$ or $(3x^2 + 7x + 4)$ or $(3x^2 + 8x + 4)$]

11. $(0, -5)$ [1]

Pages 26–29: Calculate

Complete the example

The formula for area of a trapezium is $\frac{1}{2}(a + b)h$
Substituting in the lengths from
the diagram gives $\frac{1}{2}(5\sqrt{3} - 3 + \sqrt{3} + 7) \times \sqrt{3}$
Simplifying the bracket gives $\frac{1}{2}(6\sqrt{3} + 4) \times \sqrt{3}$
Multiplying the bracket by $\frac{1}{2}$ gives $(3\sqrt{3} + 2) \times \sqrt{3}$
The area of the trapezium is $(2\sqrt{3} + 9)$ cm²

Exam practice questions

1. £140 [3]
   [1 mark for $240 \div 4.8$ or 50; 1 mark for 2.8×50 or $190 - 50$]

2. 375 [3]
   [1 mark for $\frac{b}{3 \times 5} = 2$ or $b = 30$; 1 mark for $\frac{2a}{30} = 5^2$ (or 25) or $2a = 750$]

3. 1.95 cm [5]
   [1 mark for $5 \times 28 \times 6$ or 840 or for $\pi \times r^2 \times 30$ or $30\pi r^2$ or $94.2477...r^2$; 1 mark for $1200 = 30\pi r^2 + 840$ or equivalent correct equation; 1 mark for $r^2 = (1200 - 840) \div 30\pi$ or $360 \div 94.2477...$; 1 mark for 3.81...]

4. 4.72 hours [3]
   [1 mark for Time = $(5.1 \times 10^{12}) \div (3 \times 10^8)$ or Time = 17 000 (seconds); 1 mark for $17 000 \div (60 \times 60)$]

5. 26° [3]
   [1 mark for $RNM = 180 - 125$ or 55 (co-interior or allied) or $180 - 38 - 43$ or 99 (angles in a triangle = 180°); 1 mark for $180 - 55 - 99$]

6. 5 [3]
   [1 mark for $9.6 = \frac{k}{2.5^3}$; 1 mark for $a = \frac{150}{b^3}$ or $k = 150$]

7. 5 [2]
   [1 mark for $\frac{3}{3 + y} \times \frac{3}{3 + y} = \frac{9}{25}$ or P(blue) = $\frac{3}{5}$]

8. 11.7 cm [5]

[1 mark for finding exterior or interior angle of pentagon $\frac{360}{5}$ or 72 or $180 - \frac{360}{5} = 108$ or $\frac{180(5-2)}{5}$; 1 mark for use of $\frac{1}{2}ab\sin C = 25$ to find the length of one side; 1 mark for the length of one side = 7.25…; 1 mark for use of cosine rule $EB^2 = '7.25'^2 + '7.25'^2 - 2'7.25''7.25'\cos 108$ or 137.638…

Or

1 mark for $\frac{1}{2}EB \times h = 25$; 1 mark for $\tan 54 = \frac{1}{2}\frac{EB}{h}$ and $h^2 \tan 54 = 25$; 1 mark for $h = 4.26$; 1 mark for $EB = \frac{50}{h}$]

Pages 30–31: Change / Express

Complete the example

$2\sqrt{125} = 2\sqrt{25 \times 5}$
$= 2\sqrt{25} \times \sqrt{5}$
$= 2 \times 5\sqrt{5}$
$= 10\sqrt{5}$

Exam practice questions

1. 120 000 cm² [2]

   [1 mark for $12 \times 100 \times 100$ or 12×100^2]

2. 10 (or 10^1) [2]

   [1 mark for $\sqrt{\frac{10^{10}}{10^8}}$ or $\sqrt{10^2}$]

3. 387.1 g/cm² [3]

   [1 mark for 5.5×454 or 2497; 1 mark for $2497 \div 6.45$]

4. $\frac{47}{110}$ [3]

   [1 mark for $10x = 4.2\dot{7}$ or $1000x = 427.2\dot{7}$; 1 mark for $990x = 423$ or $\frac{423}{990}$]

Pages 32–35: Simplify (fully)

Complete the example

$\frac{4(x+2)}{20} - \frac{5(x-3)}{20}$
$= \frac{4x+8}{20} - \frac{5x-15}{20}$
$= \frac{4x+8-5x+15}{20}$
$= \frac{-x+23}{20}$

Exam practice questions

1. $4x + 7$ [2]

   [1 mark for $(7x + 2) - (3x - 5)$]

2. a) $32x^{-10}$ [1]
   b) $3x^7$ [1]
   c) $2(x+y)^{-3}$ (or $\frac{2}{(x+y)^3}$) [1]
   d) $x^{-1}y^6$ [1]
   e) 1 [1]

3. $\frac{3}{2f}$ [3]

   [1 mark for $3(3f - 2g)$; 1 mark for $2f(3f - 2g)$]

4. $20a^2$ cm² [2]

   [1 mark for $\frac{1}{2}(a + 7a) \times 5a$]

5. $20\pi a^2$ m² [3]

   [1 mark for area of circular base = $\pi \times (2a)^2$ or $4\pi a^2$ or $2 \times 4\pi a^2$ or $8\pi a^2$ (in m²); 1 mark for curved surface area = $4a \times \pi \times 3a$ or $12\pi a^2$]

6. $\frac{(2x+3)}{(x+1)}$ [3]

   [1 mark for numerator of $(2x + 3)(2x - 3)$; 1 mark for denominator of $(2x - 3)(x + 1)$]

7. $\frac{4x - 11}{x - 3}$ [4]

   [1 mark for $x^2 + x - 12 = (x + 4)(x - 3)$; 1 mark for $(x + 4) \times \frac{x-2}{(x+4)(x-3)}$; 1 mark for $\frac{(x-2)}{(x-3)} + \frac{3(x-3)}{(x-3)}$ or $\frac{x-2+3x-9}{(x-3)}$]

8. 1 [2]

   [1 mark for $(5 + 3\sqrt{2})(5 - 3\sqrt{2}) = 25 - 18$ or 7]

9. $\frac{3 + \sqrt{2}}{2}$ [3]

   [1 mark for $\cos 45° = \frac{\sqrt{2}}{2}$ or $\tan 45° = 1$ or $\sin 30° = \frac{1}{2}$; 1 mark for $\frac{\sqrt{2}}{2} + 2 - \frac{1}{2}$ or $\frac{\sqrt{2}}{2} + \frac{3}{2}$]

Pages 36–39: Expand

Complete the example

Multiplying each term in the first bracket by each term in the second bracket gives

$7 \times 5 = 35$ $\qquad 7 \times 2\sqrt{3} = 14\sqrt{3}$

and

$-\sqrt{3} \times 5 = -5\sqrt{3}$ $\qquad -\sqrt{3} \times 2\sqrt{3} = -6$

Adding all the terms gives $\quad 35 + 14\sqrt{3} - 5\sqrt{3} - 6$

The final answer is $\quad 29 + 9\sqrt{3}$

Exam practice questions

1. a) $x^2 - x$ [1]
   b) -1 [1]

2. a) $5x^3 + 30x$ [2]

   [1 mark for $5x^3$ or $30x$]

   b) $2y^4 + 14y^3 + 6y^2$ [2]

   [1 mark for two correct terms from $2y^4 + 14y^3 + 6y^2$]

3. a) $y^2 + y - 20$ [2]

   [1 mark for three correct terms from $y^2 - 4y + 5y - 20$]

   b) $6x^2 - 19x - 7$ [2]

   [1 mark for three correct terms from $6x^2 + 2x - 21x - 7$]

   c) $a^2 - b^2$ [2]

   [1 mark for three correct terms from $a^2 + ab - ab - b^2$]

4. -20 [3]

   [1 mark for $6x^2 + 7x - 20$; 1 mark for $6x^2 + 7x - 20 - 6x^2 - 7x$]

5. $x^3 + 4x^2 + x - 6$ [3]

   [1 mark for the correct product of two brackets; 1 mark for at least four correct terms out of the expansion of all three brackets]

6. $2x^3 - 5x^2 - 4x + 12$ [3]

   [1 mark for $x^2 - 2x - 2x + 4$ or $2x^2 - 4x + 3x - 6$; 1 mark for the expansion of three brackets]

7. $y^3 + 14y^2 + 11y - 21$ [4]

   [1 mark for $-5y^3 + 20y$ or $-(5y^3 - 20y)$; 1 mark for $6y^3 + 14y^2 - 9y - 21$; 1 mark for $6y^3 + 14y^2 - 9y - 21 - 5y^3 + 20y$]

8. a) $21 + 8\sqrt{5}$ [2]
   [1 mark for three correct terms $16 + 4\sqrt{5} + 4\sqrt{5} + 5$]
   b) $21 - 12\sqrt{3}$ [2]
   [1 mark for three correct terms $12 - 6\sqrt{3} - 6\sqrt{3} + 9$]
9. $16x^3 - 78x^2 - 13x + 15$ [3]
   [1 mark for the correct product of two brackets; 1 mark for at least four correct terms out of the expansion of three brackets]
10. 2 [4]
    [1 mark for simplifying one radical expression, e.g. $\sqrt{\frac{1}{2}+1} = \sqrt{\frac{3}{2}}$ or $\sqrt{\frac{1}{3}+1} = \sqrt{\frac{4}{3}}$; 1 mark for $\sqrt{\frac{3}{2}} \times \sqrt{\frac{4}{3}} \times \sqrt{\frac{5}{4}} \times \sqrt{\frac{6}{5}} \times \sqrt{\frac{7}{6}} \times \sqrt{\frac{8}{7}}$ or $\sqrt{\frac{3 \times 4 \times 5 \times 6 \times 7 \times 8}{2 \times 3 \times 4 \times 5 \times 6 \times 7}}$; 1 mark for $\sqrt{\frac{8}{2}}$ or $\sqrt{4}$]

Pages 40–43: Factorise (fully)
Complete the example
$ac = -30$ $b = -13$
Two numbers that multiply to equal ac (-30) and add to equal b (-13) are -15 and 2
Rewriting the quadratic expression, replacing $-13x$ with $-15x + 2x$
$3x^2 - 15x + 2x - 10$
Now factorising the first two terms and then the second two terms separately
$3x(x - 5) + 2(x - 5)$
The final factorised answer is therefore $(3x + 2)(x - 5)$

Exam practice questions
1. a) $x(x + 6)$ [1]
   b) $5ab(3a^2 - 4b)$ [2]
      [1 mark for correct factor outside brackets: $5, a, b, 5a, 5b$ or ab]
   c) $11cd^3(2c^3d^2 - c^4d^4 + 7)$ [2]
      [1 mark for correct factor outside brackets: $11, c, d^3, 11c, 11d^3$ or cd^3]
2. a) $(a + 3)(a + 7)$ [2]
      [1 mark for $(a \pm 3)(a \pm 7)$]
   b) $(b + 5)(b - 2)$ [2]
      [1 mark for $(b \pm 5)(b \pm 2)$]
   c) $(c - 4)(c - 9)$ [2]
      [1 mark for $(c \pm 4)(c \pm 9)$]
3. a) $(a + 5)(a - 5)$ [1]
   b) $(3b + 1)(3b - 1)$ [1]
   c) $2(2c + 7)(2c - 7)$ [2]
      [1 mark for $2(4c^2 - 49)$ or $(2c \pm 7)$]
   d) $d(2d^2 + 3)(2d^2 - 3)$ [2]
      [1 mark for $d(4d^4 - 9)$ or $(2d^3 + 3d)(2d^2 - 3)$ or $(2d^2 + 3)(2d^3 - 3d)$]
4. a) $(3h + 1)(h - 4)$ [2]
      [1 mark for $(3h \pm 1)(h \pm 4)$]
   b) $(3g - 2)(2g - 3)$ [2]
      [1 mark for $(3g \pm 2)(2g \pm 3)$]

5. $(\frac{1}{2}x + 1)(\frac{1}{2}x + 2)$ [2]
   [1 mark for $(\frac{1}{2}x \pm 1)(\frac{1}{2}x \pm 2)$]
   Alternative answer: $\frac{1}{4}(x + 4)(x + 2)$ [2]
   [1 mark for $\frac{1}{4}(x^2 + 6x + 8)$]
6. $(x + \sqrt{2})(x + \sqrt{2})$ or $(x + \sqrt{2})^2$ [2]
   [1 mark for $(x \pm \sqrt{2})(x \pm \sqrt{2})$ or $(x \pm \sqrt{2})^2$]
7. $(5x - 3y)(x - 2y)$ [2]
   [1 mark for $(5x \pm 3y)(x \pm 2y)$]

Pages 44–47: Solve / Make … the subject of the formula
Complete the example
Multiplying both sides by $(x - 2)$ gives $y(x - 2) = 3x + 8$
Expanding the brackets $xy - 2y = 3x + 8$
Rearranging to move the x terms to the left-hand side and the numbers to the right-hand side $xy - 3x = 8 + 2y$
Factorising $x(y - 3) = 8 + 2y$
Dividing both sides by the bracket $x = \frac{8 + 2y}{y - 3}$

Exam practice questions
1. $x = \frac{3y + 20}{4}$ or $x = \frac{3y}{4} + 5$ [2]
   [1 mark for $4x = 3y + 20$ or $x - 5 = \frac{3y}{4}$]
2. $x = 2$ or $x = -16$ [3]
   [1 mark for $(x \pm 2)(x \pm 16)$; 1 mark for $(x - 2)(x + 16)$]
3. $x = \frac{1}{2}$, $y = -2$ [4]
   [1 mark for eliminating either x or y to get $5y = -10$ or $5x = \frac{5}{2}$; 1 mark for either $y = -2$ or $x = \frac{1}{2}$; 1 mark for correct substitution into one equation to find second answer]
4. $x = 3.2$ [2]
   [1 mark for $60.8 = 19x$ or $-60.8 = -19x$]
5. $x > -\frac{14}{5}$ [2]
   [1 mark for $5x > -14$]
6. $x = 3.58$ or $x = 0.42$ [3]
   [1 mark for substituting into formula $\frac{8 \pm \sqrt{(-8)^2 - (4 \times 2 \times 3)}}{2 \times 2}$ or for attempt to complete the square; 1 mark for $\frac{8 \pm \sqrt{40}}{4}$ or $\frac{4 \pm \sqrt{10}}{2}$]
7. $x = \frac{3y - 1}{1 + 2y}$ [4]
   [1 mark for $y(3 - 2x) = x + 1$ or $3y - 2xy = x + 1$; 1 mark for $3y - 1 = x + 2xy$; 1 mark for $3y - 1 = x(1 + 2y)$]
8. $x > 6$ or $x < 0$ [2]
   [1 mark for $x^2 - 6x > 0$ or $x(x - 6) > 0$]
9. $x = 9$ or $x = -3$ [3]
   [1 mark for $(x - 3)^2 \pm \ldots$; 1 mark for $(x - 3)^2 - 9 - 27$ or $(x - 3)^2 - 36$ or $(x - 3)^2 = 36$]
10. $x = 4$ or $x = \frac{1}{2}$ [4]
    [1 mark for $2(x + 1) + 3(2x - 3) = (2x - 3)(x + 1)$; 1 mark for $2x + 2 + 6x - 9 = 2x^2 + 2x - 3x - 3$ or $8x - 7 = 2x^2 - x - 3$; 1 mark for $2x^2 - 9x + 4$ or $(2x - 1)(x - 4)$]

Pages 48–51: Match (each graph) / Mark

Complete the example

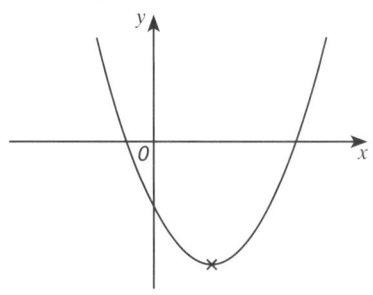

A is $y = 2^x$
B is $y = -x^2 - 2$
C is $y = x^3$
D is $y = \sin x$

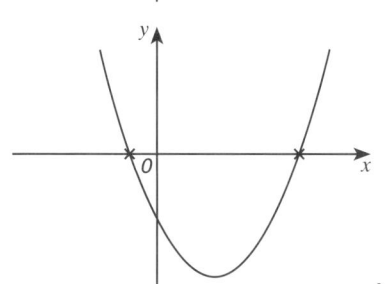

Exam practice questions

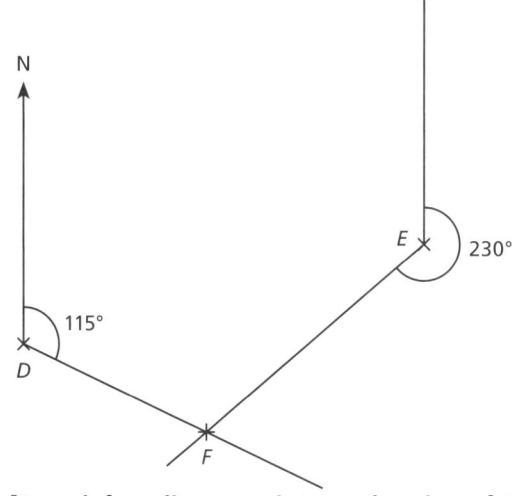

1. a) [1]

   b) [1]

2. [3]

   [1 mark for a line or point on a bearing of 115° from D; 1 mark for a line or point on a bearing of 230° from E]

3.

Proportionality relationship	Graph
y is directly proportional to x	C
y is inversely proportional to x	B
y is proportional to the square of x	D
y is inversely proportional to the square of x	A

[2]

[1 mark for at least two correct]

4.

Equation	Graph
$y = \cos x$	D
$y = 2^{-x}$	A
$y = 2x - 3$	F
$y = -\dfrac{1}{x}$	B
$y = x^2 - 3$	C

[3]

[2 marks for at least three correct; 1 mark for at least two correct]

Pages 52–55: Complete

Complete the example

Height, h (m)	≤1	≤2	≤3	≤4	≤5
Frequency	17	39	66	79	90

Exam practice questions

1. $67.45 \leq n < 67.55$ [2]

   [1 mark for a 67.45 in the correct position; 1 mark for 67.55 in the correct position]

2.

	Square	Circle	Triangle	Total
Blue	12	24	24	60
Red	13	18	12	43
Total	25	42	36	103

All correct [4]

[1 mark for blue circles : red circles : blue squares = 24 : 18 : 12; 1 mark for total blue shapes = 60; 1 mark for red squares = 13]

3.

Profit (£p)	Frequency
$0 < p \leq 150$	4
$0 < p \leq 300$	25
$0 < p \leq 450$	53
$0 < p \leq 600$	69
$0 < p \leq 750$	77
$0 < p \leq 900$	80

[1]

4.

Least height	18 cm
Lower quartile	24 cm
Interquartile range	26 cm
Median	33 cm
Range	41 cm

[3]

[2 marks for at least three correct values; 1 mark for two correct values]

5.

nth term	1st term	2nd term	5th term	10th term
$2n^2 - 2$	0	6	48	198
$4n + 1$	5	9	21	41
$\dfrac{1}{n}$	1	$\dfrac{1}{2}$	$\dfrac{1}{5}$	$\dfrac{1}{10}$
$7 - n^3$	6	−1	−118	−993

All correct [4]

[1 mark for each correct row]

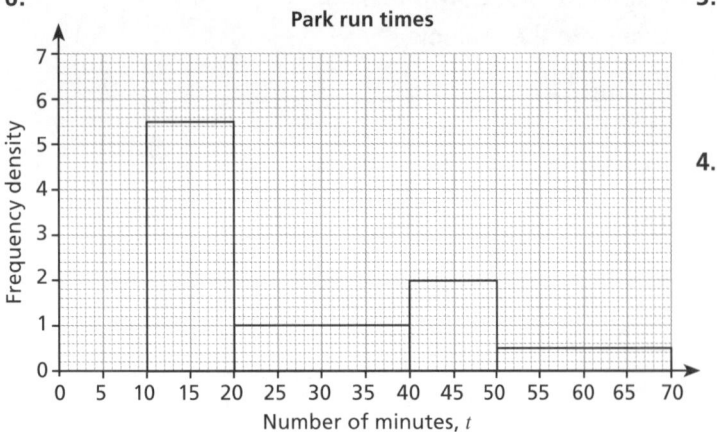

6.

Park run times [graph]

[4]

[1 mark for 10 × 5.5 = 55 or 20 × 1 = 20 or 10 × 2 = 20;
1 mark for 105 − 55 − 20 − 20 or 10; 1 mark for 10 ÷ 20 or 0.5]

7.

x	−2	−1	0	1	2	3
y	1.25	**1.5**	**2**	3	**5**	9

[2]

[1 mark for two or three correct values]

Pages 56–59: Estimate
Complete the example

Speed (s miles per hour)	Class width	Frequency density	Frequency	Cumulative frequency
$10 < s \leqslant 20$	10	0.7	7	7
$20 < s \leqslant 25$	5	1	**5**	12
$25 < s \leqslant 30$	5	3	15	**27**
$30 < s \leqslant 45$	15	0.6	9	**36**

So the median lies in the interval **25 < s ⩽ 30**

Median = $25 + \frac{6}{15} \times 5$
= **27** mph

Exam practice questions

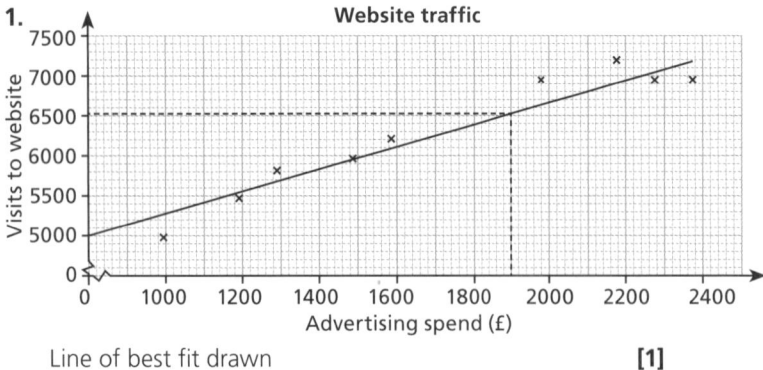

1. Website traffic [scatter graph]

Line of best fit drawn [1]
Lines drawn to/from the x- and y-axes [1]
Answer between 6400 and 6600 [1]

2. Either 812.4 rounded to 810 or 30.2 rounded to 30 [1]
$\frac{30 \times x^2}{3} = 810 \Rightarrow 10x^2 = 810 \Rightarrow x^2 = 81$ [1]
$x = 9$ [1]

3. Total number sampled =
600 + 500 + 900 + 800 + 700 = 3500 [1]
Total number faulty = 54 + 48 + 99 + 84 + 82 = 367 [1]
Relative frequency of faulty = $\frac{367}{3500}$ [1]

4. Sea turtles [cumulative frequency graph]

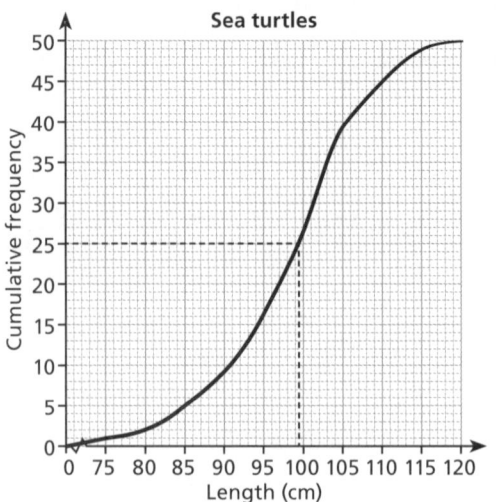

Lines drawn from axes [1]
Answer between 99–100 cm [1]

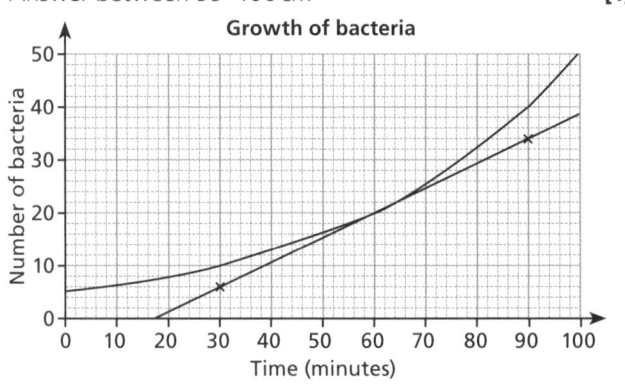

5. Growth of bacteria [graph]

Tangent drawn on curve at $x = 60$ [1]
Finding gradient from two points that are on the line,
e.g. (30, 6) and (90, 34) [1]
$m = \frac{34 - 6}{90 - 30} = \frac{28}{60}$
= 0.47 bacteria per minute (to 2 d.p.) [1]

Pages 60–65: Draw / Sketch

Complete the example

Height, x (cm)	Frequency	Class width	Frequency density
$40 \leq x < 50$	15	10	$15 \div 10 = 1.5$
$50 \leq x < 65$	30	15	$30 \div 15 = 2$
$65 \leq x < 75$	30	10	$30 \div 10 = 3$
$75 \leq x < 80$	10	5	$10 \div 5 = 2$

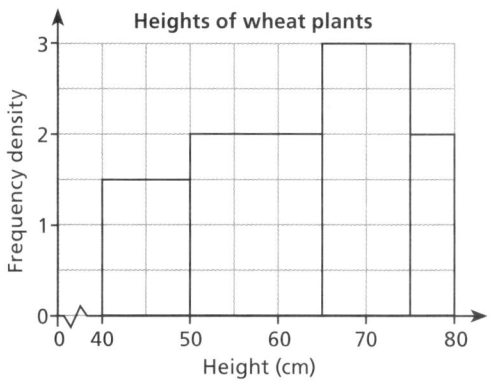

Exam practice questions

1. Sketch of a cylinder with 6 cm diameter (or 3 cm radius) and a height of 7 cm. [2]
   [1 mark for a sketch of a cylinder]

2. A triangle drawn with a base of 3 and a height of 6 in any orientation and anywhere on the grid. [2]

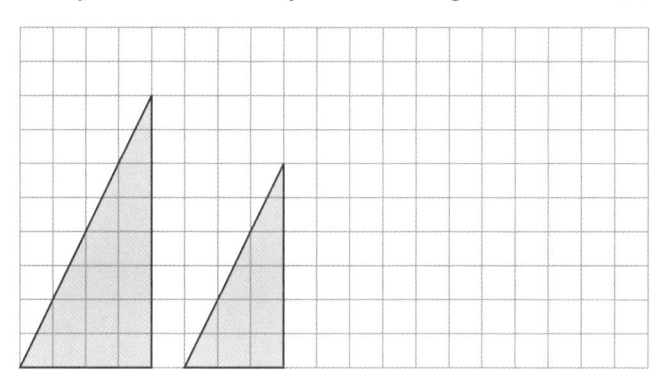

   [1 mark for only one of the base or height correct]

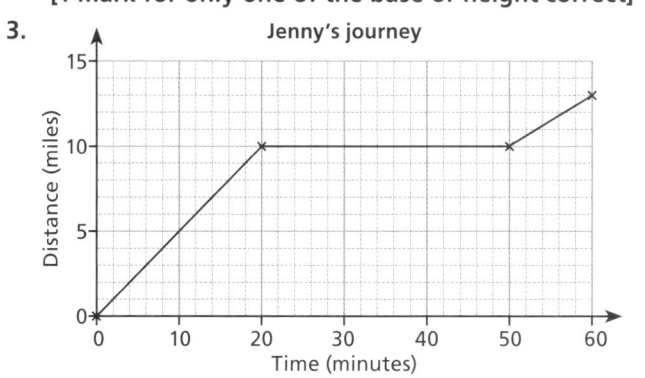

3. Fully correct [3]
   [1 mark for line from (0, 0) to (20, 10); 1 mark for horizontal line from (20, 10) to (50, 10); 1 mark for line from (50, 10) to (60, 13)]

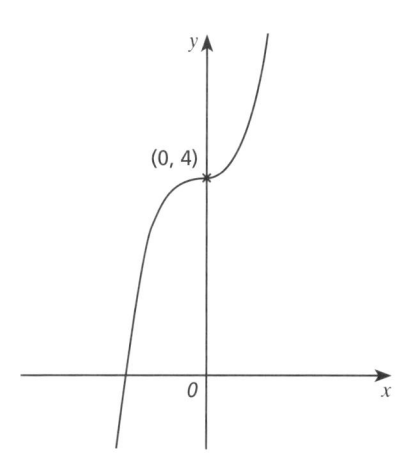

4. Fully correct [2]
   [1 mark for correct shape of cubic graph; 1 mark for point (0, 4) labelled]

5.

Mass, x (kg)	Number of cats	Cumulative frequency
$3.0 < x \leq 3.5$	3	3
$3.5 < x \leq 4.0$	8	11
$4.0 < x \leq 4.5$	15	26
$4.5 < x \leq 5.0$	10	36
$5.0 < x \leq 5.5$	4	40

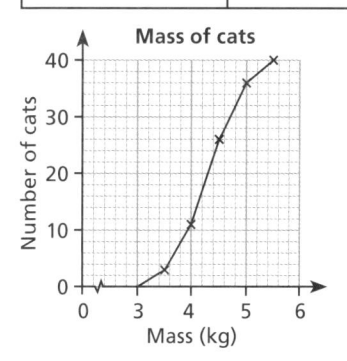

Fully correct [3]
[1 mark for correct cumulative frequencies calculated; 1 mark for points plotted at upper value of class interval; 1 mark for points connected with a smooth curved line or straight lines]

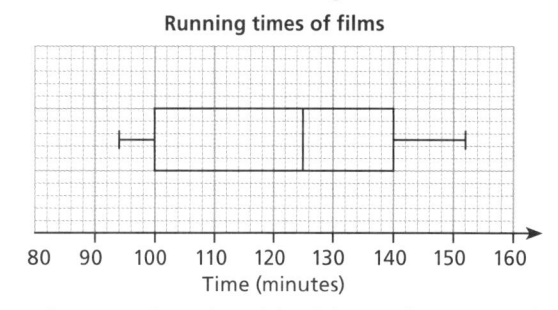

6. Fully correct box plot with minimum, lower quartile, median, upper quartile and maximum shown [3]
[2 marks for at least four of these values correctly shown; 1 mark for at least three of these values correctly shown]

7.

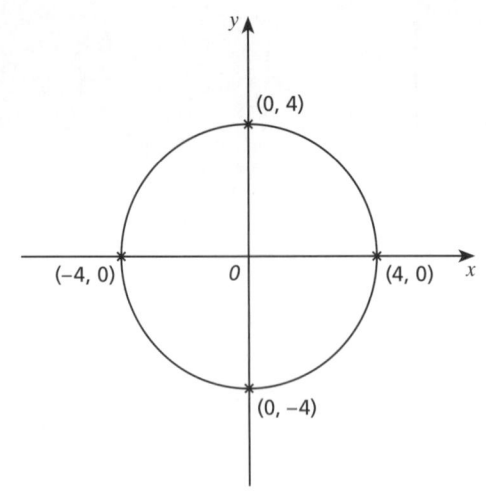

Fully correct [2]

[1 mark for circle with centre (0, 0); 1 mark for at least one point correctly labelled indicating a radius of 4 at (0, 4), (4, 0), (−4, 0) or (0, −4)]

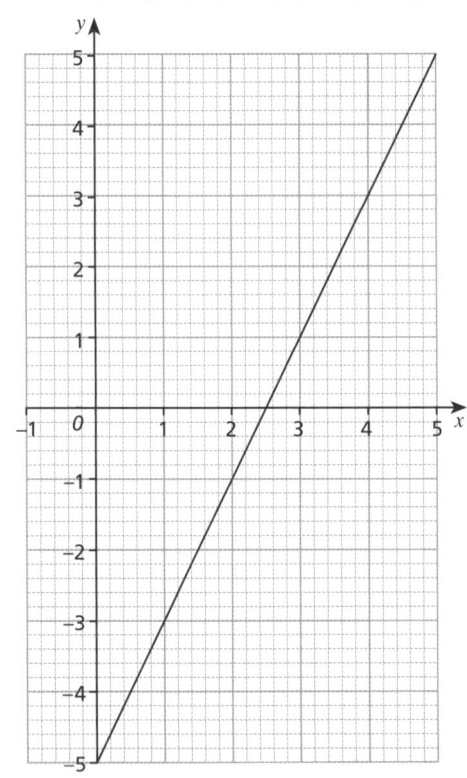

Points labelled: (0, 4), (−4, 0), (4, 0), (0, −4)

8.

Fully correct [2]

[1 mark for fg(x) = 2x − 5 seen but line not drawn]

Note: fg(x) = f(x − 3) = 2(x − 3) + 1
fg(x) = 2x − 6 + 1
= 2x − 5

Pages 66–69: Is … correct?
Complete the example

Area of bar between 160 ⩽ height < 200 cm is 12 × **10** = **120** square units
Area of bar between 200 ⩽ height < 220 cm is 16 × **5** = **80** square units
Area of bar between 220 ⩽ height < 240 cm is **8** × 5 = **40** square units
There are more sunflowers between **160** cm ⩽ height < **200** cm
No, he is not correct.

Exam practice questions

1. Yes, they are congruent by side-angle-side (SAS) [1]
2. Yes
   2 : 5 → 100 : 250 [1]
   She has 100 ml of juice, which she would need to mix with 250 ml of water, so she can make 350 ml of the drink. [1]
3. No, $5^3 \times 5^6 = 5^9$
   By the laws of indices, $a^m \times a^n = a^{(m+n)}$ [1]
4. Yes
   Q1 = 8.5 and Q3 = 14, hence interquartile range is
   14 − 8.5 = 5.5 [1]
5. No
   $x = 0.454545…$ **and** $100x = 45.454545…$ [1]
   $99x = 45$ **and** $x = \frac{45}{99}$ [1]
6. Yes
   $\frac{2}{3} \times 30 = 20$ and $0.4 \times 30 = 12$ [1]

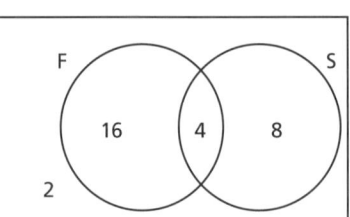

   Venn diagram: F contains 16, intersection 4, S contains 8, outside 2

   [1]
   $P(S|F) = \frac{4}{20} = 20\%$ [1]
7. No
   Method of completing the square.
   $(x − 5)^2 − 5^2 + 28$ **or** $(x − 5)^2 − 25 + 28$ **or** $(x − 5)^2 + 3$ [2]
   [1 mark for $(x − 5)^2$; 1 mark for the rest of the expression]
   Turning point is at $x = 5$ / Turning point has coordinates (5, 3) [1]

Pages 70–75: Use (a given method)
Complete the example

To work out the speed at 2 seconds, draw the **tangent** to the curve at $x = $ **2**.
Then work out the gradient of the tangent.
Make a right-angled triangle.
Point (0, **4**) and (2, **10**) are on the tangent.
$\frac{10 − 4}{2 − 0} = \frac{6}{2} = 3$
The speed is **3** m/s.

Exam practice questions

1. Using Pythagoras' theorem with 5 cm as the base.
   $a^2 = 13^2 − 5^2$ [1]
   $a = \sqrt{144} = 12$, so $h = 12$ cm [1]
2. $C = \left(\frac{5}{9}\right)(F − 32)$ [1]
   $C = \left(\frac{5}{9}\right)(100 − 32) = 37.\dot{7} = 38°C$ [1]
3. $\frac{\sqrt{100 − 3^2}}{0.5 + 3}$ [1]
   $= \frac{(10 − 9)}{(3.5)} = \frac{1}{3.5}$ [1]
   $= \frac{2}{7}$ [1]
   [2 marks for correct rounding of all numbers; 1 mark for at least one correct rounding]

4. Suitable line of best fit drawn, e.g. [1]

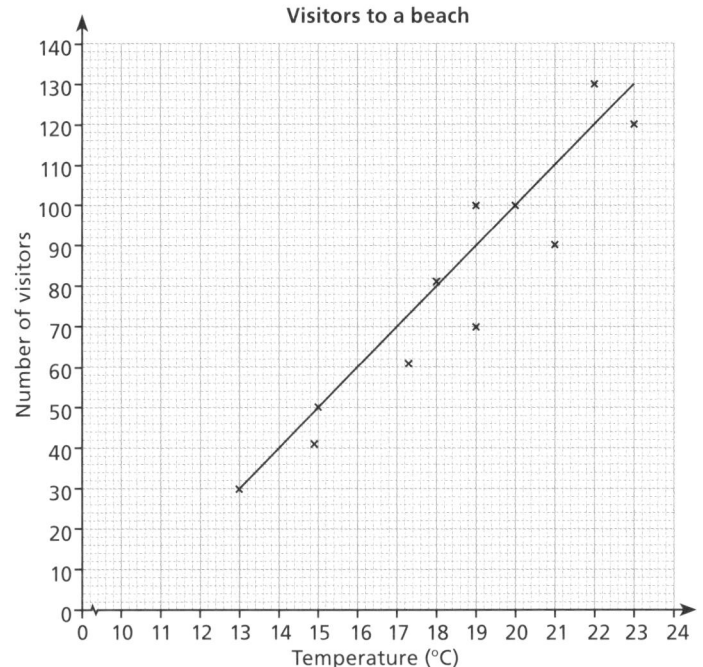

Visitors to a beach

Any suitable answer read off line of best fit at 16°C, e.g. 60 visitors **[accept any answer in range 58–62]** [1]

5.

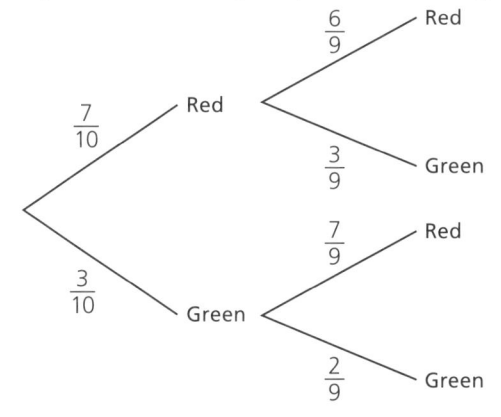

At least two of the probabilities from $\frac{6}{9}, \frac{2}{9}, \frac{7}{9}, \frac{3}{9}$ seen [1]

$\left(\frac{7}{10} \times \frac{3}{9}\right) + \left(\frac{3}{10} \times \frac{7}{9}\right)$ [1]

$= \frac{7}{15}$ [1]

6. End of September has 500 cumulative sales
End of April has 125 cumulative sales
$500 - 125 = 375$ [1]
$\frac{375}{530} = \frac{75}{106}$ or 71% [1]

7. $\frac{\sin x}{12} = \frac{\sin 60}{15}$ [1]

$x = \sin^{-1}\left(\frac{12 \sin 60}{15}\right)$ [1]

$x = 43.8537... = 44°$ [1]

8. $4x^2 + 8x + 5 = -4x - 4$ [1]
$4x^2 + 12x + 9 = 0$ [1]
$D = \sqrt{12^2 - (4 \times 4 \times 9)} = \sqrt{144 - 144} = 0$ [1]
The discriminant is zero, so there is one solution [1]

Alternative method:
$4x^2 + 8x + 5 = -4x - 4$ [1]
$4x^2 + 12x + 9 = 0$ [1]
$(2x + 3)^2 = 0$ [1]
$x = -\frac{3}{2}$ so there is one solution [1]

9. $(x - 4)^2 - 16 + 5 = 0$ [1]
$(x - 4)^2 = 11$ [1]
$x - 4 = \pm \sqrt{11}$ [1]
$x = 4 \pm \sqrt{11}$ [1]

Pages 76–79: Translate / Reflect / Rotate / Enlarge

Complete the example

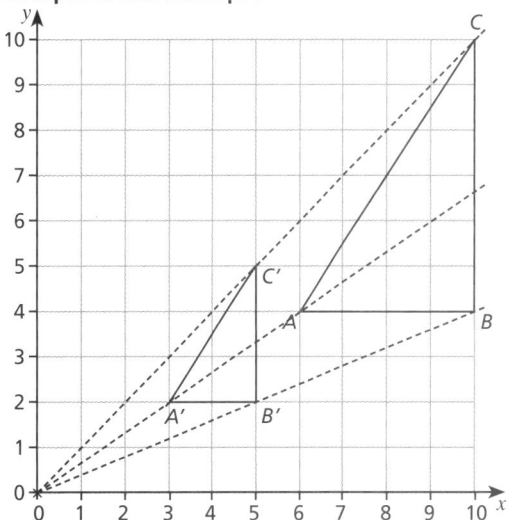

Exam practice questions

1. [2]

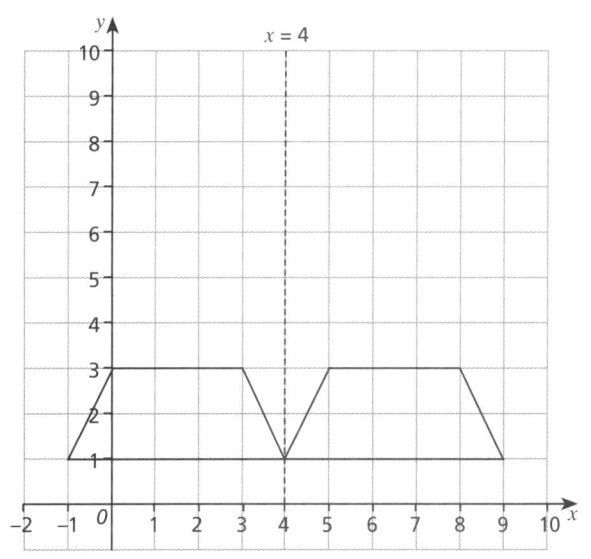

[1 mark for correct size and orientation in wrong position]

2. [2]

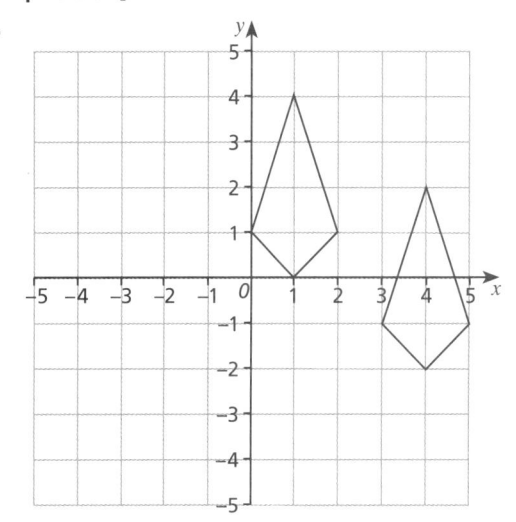

[1 mark for correct size and orientation in wrong position]

3.

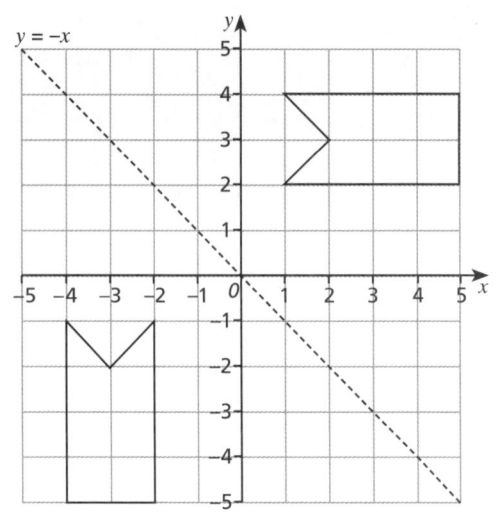

[1 mark for correct size and orientation in wrong position]

4.

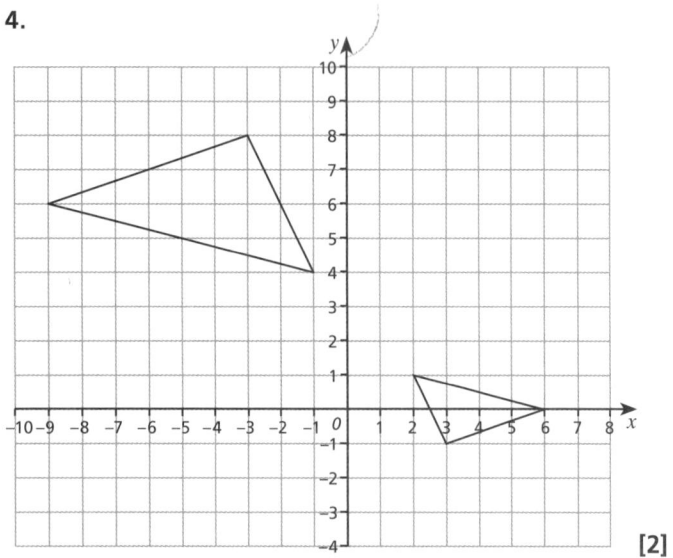

[1 mark for correct size and orientation in wrong position]

Pages 80–85: Describe
Complete the example

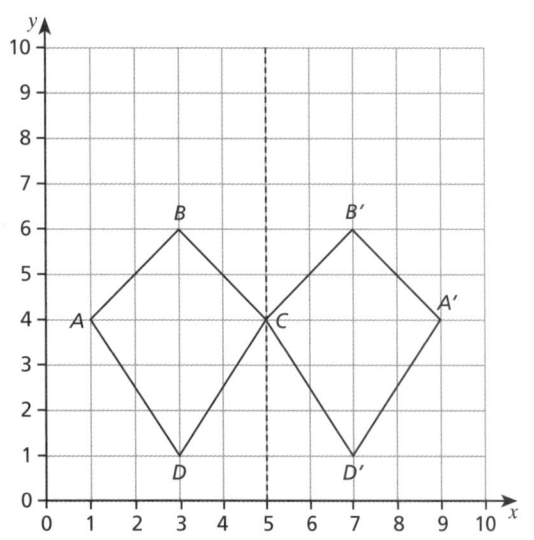

Kite ABCD has been **reflected** in the line $x = 5$

Exam practice questions
1. a) *Any one from*: multiply by 2 / double [1]
   b) *Any one from*: geometric / geometrical progression [1]

2. Enlargement [1]
   with a scale factor of $\frac{1}{2}$ [1]
   about the point (2, 0) [1]
3. Number of sides [1]
4. The value of y quarters / divides by 4 [1]
5. The median is 13 [1]
   The interquartile range is $14 - 11 = 3$ [1]
6. $y \leq 5$ [1]
   $y > x^2 - x - 2$ [1]
7. Translation [1]
   Vector $\begin{pmatrix} 4 \\ 0 \end{pmatrix}$ [1]

Pages 86–91: Construct
Complete the example

Using the scale of 1 cm to 5 m, 20 m is **4** cm on the map.
Draw a circle with radius of **4** cm around the tree.
To identify the area that is nearer to the playground than the football pitch, construct the **angle bisector** of angle ADC.
Label the region **outside** the circle and to the left of the **angle bisector** as R.

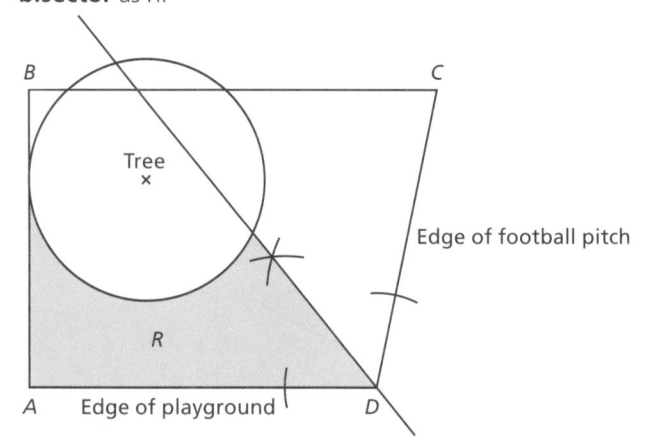

Exam practice questions
1.

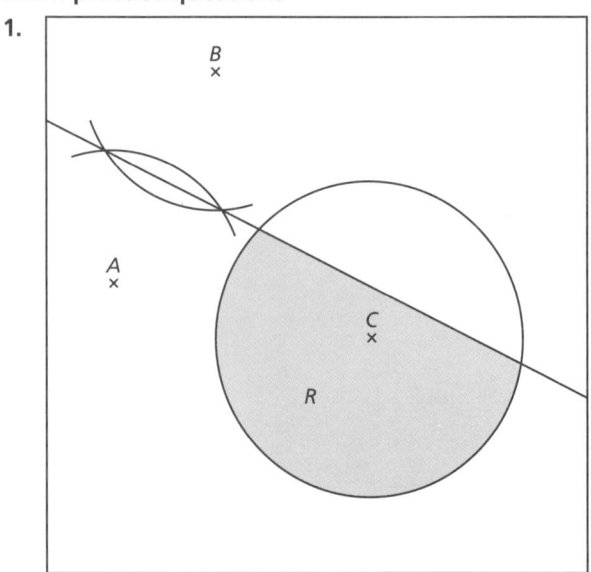

Circle of radius 3 cm around C [1]
Arcs of equal radii drawn from point A and B and perpendicular bisector drawn [1]
Correct region labelled [1]

2.

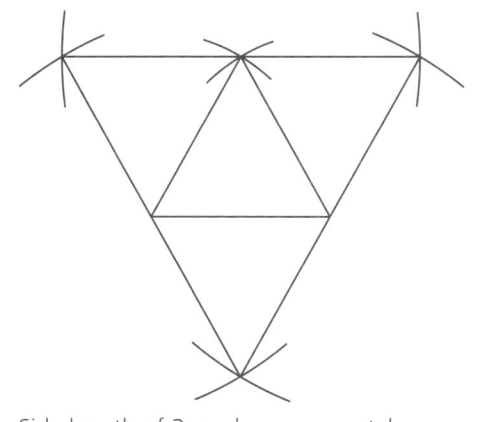

Side length of 3 cm drawn accurately [1]
Arcs of 3 cm radii shown on all triangles [1]
Correct net [1]

3.

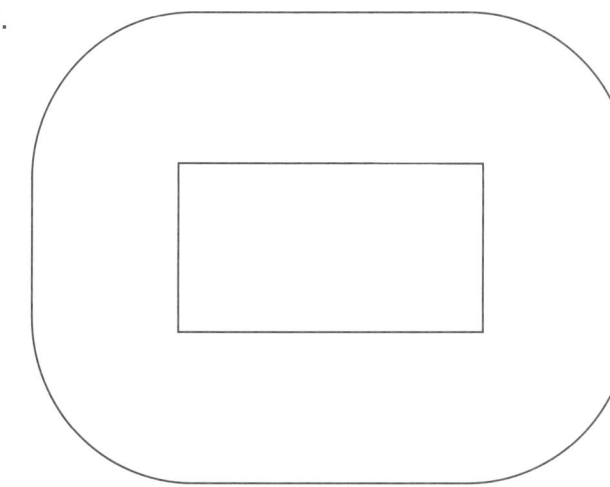

Straight lines 2 cm from rectangle [1]
Quadrants, radius 2 cm at the corners [1]

4.

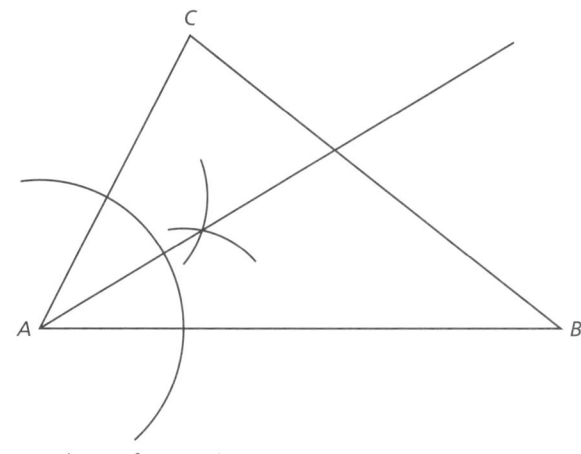

Arc drawn from point A [1]
Intersecting arcs of equal radii [1]
Angle bisector drawn [1]

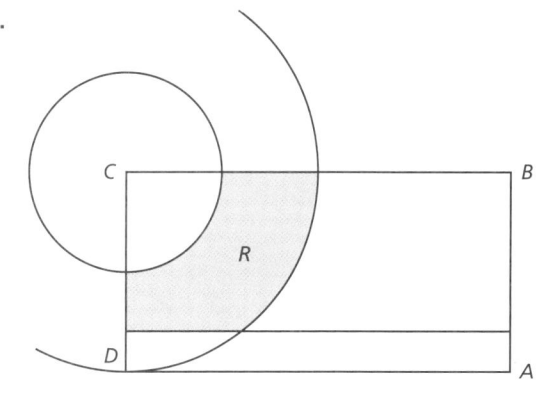

5.

Line drawn 1 cm from AD [1]
Circles drawn 2.5 cm and 5 cm from C [1]
Correct region shaded [1]

Pages 92–95: Give your answer
Complete the example
Mass = Volume × Density
Mass = 642.5 × 19.3
Mass = **12 400.25** grams
Mass = **12.4** kg (to 1 d.p.)

Exam practice questions

1. $2^3 \times 3^2$ [2]
   [1 mark for 2 × 2 × 2 × 3 × 3]
2. $3\frac{1}{15}$ [3]
   [2 marks for $\frac{46}{15}$ or $\frac{23}{5} \times \frac{2}{3}$; 1 mark for $\frac{23}{5} \div \frac{3}{2}$]
3. a) 9 [2]
   [1 mark for 3^2]
   b) 7^5 [2]
   [1 mark for $\frac{7^8}{7^3}$]
4. 975 grams [2]
   [1 mark for identifying 0.75 kg and 1 kilogram 200 grams as middle values, e.g. four masses ordered or $\frac{750 + 1200}{2}$]
5. $\frac{15}{28}$ [2]
   [1 mark for $\frac{6}{8} \times \frac{5}{7}$ or $\frac{30}{56}$]
6. $(\sqrt{3} + \sqrt{6})(\sqrt{3} + \sqrt{6}) = 3 + \sqrt{18} + \sqrt{18} + 6 = 9 + 2\sqrt{18}$ [1]
   $\sqrt{18} = \sqrt{2 \times 9} = 3\sqrt{2}$ [1]
   $(\sqrt{3} + \sqrt{6})^2 = 9 + 2 \times 3\sqrt{2} = 9 + 6\sqrt{2}$ [1]
7. $x_2 = -0.8$ [1]
   $x_3 = -0.5882...$ [1]
   $x_4 = -0.6071..., x_5 = -0.6054..., x_6 = -0.6055...,$
   $x_7 = -0.6055...$ [1]
   $-0.606...$ (3 s.f.) [1]
8. $\vec{BC} = \vec{BA} + \vec{AC} = -\mathbf{a} + 2\mathbf{b}$ [1]
   $\vec{SC} = \frac{2}{5}(-\mathbf{a} + 2\mathbf{b}) = -\frac{2}{5}\mathbf{a} + \frac{4}{5}\mathbf{b}$ [1]
   $\vec{SR} = \vec{SC} + \vec{CR} = -\frac{2}{5}\mathbf{a} + \frac{4}{5}\mathbf{b} - \mathbf{b}$ [1]
   $\vec{SR} = -\frac{2}{5}\mathbf{a} - \frac{1}{5}\mathbf{b}$ [1]
9. $BC^2 = 15^2 + 17^2 - 2 \times 15 \times 17 \times \cos 54°$ [1]
   $BC = \sqrt{15^2 + 17^2 - 2 \times 15 \times 17 \times \cos 54°}$ [1]
   $BC = 14.636...$
   $BC = 14.6$ cm or $BC = 15$ cm [1]

10. $x = \dfrac{-(-5) \pm \sqrt{(-5)^2 - 4(2)(-6)}}{2 \times 2}$ [1]

$x = \dfrac{5 \pm \sqrt{25 + 48}}{4} = \dfrac{5 \pm \sqrt{73}}{4}$ [1]

$x = 3.39$ or $x = -0.89$ (to 2 d.p.) [1]

Pages 96–101: Give a reason
Complete the example
Angle A + Angle B = $5x$ and Angle C + Angle D = **$5x$**
This means that Angle A + Angle B = 180° and
Angle C + Angle D = **180°**
So AD is parallel to **BC**, meaning that shape ABCD is a trapezium.

Exam practice questions
1. a) All square numbers have a repeated factor [1]
   b) Negative × negative = positive, and positive × positive = positive [1]
2. The terms of the linear sequence are all odd; the terms of the geometric sequence are all even [1]
3. $2^2 \times 3 \times 5^2$ is the HCF of A and B [1]
   The LCM of A and B is $2^3 \times 3 \times 5^2 \times 7$ [1]
4. He is correct. Possible transformations are:
   Reflection in the line $y = -x$ [1]
   Rotation 180° about O [1]
5. a) There is a fixed charge of £10 [1]
   b) Hiring up to 5 hours with Cyclesafely is cheaper, then it is more expensive [1]
   This could be shown on the graph.

6. Using the measurements to 1 decimal place will give the more accurate answer as using lengths closer to accurate length [1]
7. Angle between a tangent and radius is always 90° [1]
8. The volumes are in the ratio $1^3 : 2^3 = 1 : 8$
   The volumes are in the ratio 1 : 8 is correct [1]
   Note: The lengths are in the ratio 3 : 6 = 1 : 2
   The (surface) areas are in the ratio $1^2 : 2^2 = 1 : 4$
9. It is an underestimate as gives area of triangle (as shown). [1]

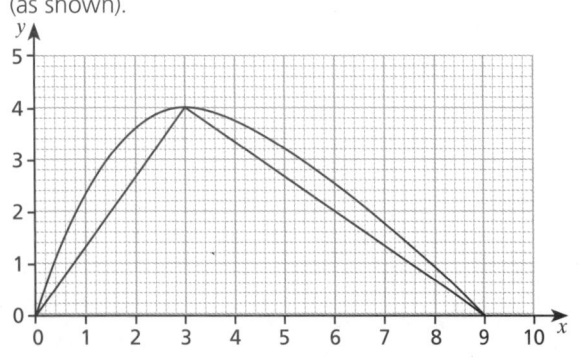

10. a) Angle BCD = 180° − 116° = 64° [1]
    Opposite angles of a cyclic quadrilateral add up to 180° [1]
    b) Angle BOD = 64° × 2 = 128° [1]
    Angle subtended by an arc at the centre of a circle is twice the angle subtended at any point on the circumference. [1]

Pages 102–105: Explain / Justify
Complete the example
The probability of getting a score of 11 $P(11) = P(5) \times P(6) \times 2$
$= \dfrac{1}{6} \times \dfrac{1}{6} \times 2 = \dfrac{1}{18}$

Exam practice questions
1. a) Correct answer is 1.23×10^6 [1]
   b) Correct answer is 4.56×10^{-3} [1]
   Note: Standard form should be in the form $A \times 10^n$, where $1 \leq A < 10$
2. Yes, Yuri is correct. The higher weekly wages affect the calculation of the mean.
   (The mode or median may be a better average to use.) [1]
3. Benji is wrong because most of the points on the scatter diagram do follow the line of best fit. (It is a negative correlation.) [1]
4. LCM of (3 + 7) and (5 + 2) is 70, or
   There is no smaller multiple of 10 and 7 (than 70) [1]
5. Using a broken axis means that bars are misleading (as not in proportion) [1]
   Vertical scale should be labelled 'Frequency density' [1]
6. $27^{-\frac{1}{3}}$ means the reciprocal of $\sqrt[3]{27}$, which is $\dfrac{1}{3}$ [2]
   [1 mark for $\sqrt[3]{27} = 3$ or $\dfrac{1}{27^{\frac{1}{3}}}$ or $\dfrac{1}{\sqrt[3]{27}}$]

Pages 106–111: Prove that / Show (that)
Complete the example
Let x be any integer.
So any odd numbers would be of the form $2x + 1$
(odd number)^2 can be written as $(2x + 1)^2$
Expanding the expression $(2x + 1)(2x + 1) = 4x^2 + 2x + \mathbf{2x + 1}$
Simplifying $= 4x^2 + \mathbf{4x + 1}$
$= 4(x^2 + x) + \mathbf{1}$
$4(x^2 + x)$ must be even as any multiple of 4 is even.
So $4(x^2 + x) + \mathbf{1}$ is always **odd**.

Exam practice questions
1. a) Perimeter $= 6x + x + 5 + 5x - 1 + 4x = (16x + 4)$ cm [1]
   b) If $x = 1.5$, $6x = 9$, $5x - 1 = 6.5$, $x + 5 = 6.5$, $4x = 6$ [1]
   $(5x - 1)$ cm and $(x + 5)$ cm are the same lengths [1]
2. 40 − 12 = 28 [1]
   28 divided in the ratio 5 : 2 gives
   28 ÷ 7 × 5 : 28 ÷ 7 × 2 = 20 : 8 [1]
   Missing value is 12 + 20 or 40 − 8 = 32 [1]
3. a) Perimeter $= x + 1.5h + x + 1.5h = (2x + 3h) = 28$ [1]
   b) If $x = 8$, $(16 + 3h) = 28$ [1]
   $3h = 12$, $h = 4$ [1]
   Area $= 8 \times 4 = 32$ cm^2 [1]
4. $(n + 1)^2 + (n - 1)^2 = n^2 + 2n + 1 + n^2 - 2n + 1$ [2]
   [1 mark for each expansion]
   $= 2n^2 + 2 = 2(n^2 + 1)$, so multiple of 2 so always even [1]

5. $10^2 = AC^2 + 6^2$ or $100 = AC^2 + 36$ [1]
    $AC^2 = 100 - 36$ or $AC^2 = 64$ [1]
    $AC = 8$ cm [1]
    Area $= \frac{1}{2} \times 12 \times 8 = 48$ cm^2 [1]
6. Ratio of lengths $= 2 : 7$, so ratio of surface areas
    $= 2^2 : 7^2$ or $4 : 49 = 1 : 12.25$ [2]
    [1 mark for $2^2 : 7^2$ or $4 : 49$]
7. a) $2\sin 45°\cos 45° = 2 \times \frac{1}{\sqrt{2}} \times \frac{1}{\sqrt{2}}$ or $2\sin 45° \cos 45°$
    $= 2 \times \frac{\sqrt{2}}{2} \times \frac{\sqrt{2}}{2}$ [1]
    $= 1 = \sin 90°$ [1]
    b) $2\sin 30°\cos 30° = 2 \times \frac{1}{2} \times \frac{\sqrt{3}}{2}$ [2]
    [1 mark for $\sin 30° = \frac{1}{2}$ or $\cos 30° = \frac{\sqrt{3}}{2}$]
    $= \frac{\sqrt{3}}{2} = \sin 60°$ [1]
8. $(4n + 3)^2 - (4n - 3)^2 = 16n^2 + 24n + 9 - (16n^2 - 24n + 9)$ [2]
    [1 mark for each expansion]
    $= 48n$, so a multiple of 8 [1]
9. $y = 30 - 4x$
    At point of intersection, $x^2 + 6 = 30 - 4x$
    $x^2 + 4x - 24 = 0$ [2]
    [1 mark for $y = 30 - 4x$]
10. If there are 15 green counters, there will be
    5 red counters. [1]
    P(red, red, red) $= \frac{5}{20} \times \frac{4}{19} \times \frac{3}{18} = \frac{1}{4} \times \frac{4}{19} \times \frac{1}{6} = \frac{1}{114}$
    So 15 green counters in the bag. [1]
11. $(\sqrt{2} + \sqrt{6})^2 = (\sqrt{2} + \sqrt{6})(\sqrt{2} + \sqrt{6}) = 2 + \sqrt{12} + \sqrt{12} + 6$
    $= 2 + \sqrt{4 \times 3} + \sqrt{4 \times 3} + 6 = 2 + 2\sqrt{3} + 2\sqrt{3} + 6 =$
    $8 + 4\sqrt{3}$ [1]
    $(2 + \sqrt{3})^2 = (2 + \sqrt{3})(2 + \sqrt{3}) = 4 + 2\sqrt{3} + 2\sqrt{3} + 3$
    $= 7 + 4\sqrt{3}$ [1]
    $(\sqrt{2} + \sqrt{6})^2 - (2 + \sqrt{3})^2 = (8 + 4\sqrt{3}) - (7 + 4\sqrt{3}) = 1$ [1]
12. a) $u_2 = 6u_1 - 5 = 6(2) - 5 = 12 - 5 = 7$ [1]
    b) $u_{n+2} = 6u_{n+1} - 5$ [1]
    $= 6(6u_n - 5) - 5 = 36u_n - 30 - 5 = 36u_n - 35$ [1]
13. Any two of:
    $\overrightarrow{AB} = \overrightarrow{AO} + \overrightarrow{OB} = -\mathbf{a} + \mathbf{b}$
    $\overrightarrow{AP} = \overrightarrow{AO} + \overrightarrow{OP} = -\mathbf{a} - 4\mathbf{a} + 5\mathbf{b} = -5\mathbf{a} + 5\mathbf{b}$
    $\overrightarrow{BP} = \overrightarrow{BO} + \overrightarrow{OP} = -\mathbf{b} - 4\mathbf{a} + 5\mathbf{b} = -4\mathbf{a} + 4\mathbf{b}$
    For example, $\overrightarrow{AB}$ is a multiple of $\overrightarrow{AP}$ [3]
    [Marks are for working out any two of the vectors in terms of a and b and then recognising that they are a multiple of each other]

Pages 112–119: Mixed questions

1. a) n^2, 2^n, $16n^0$ and $4n$ (all equal 16) [3]
    [2 marks for correct substitution of $n = 4$ into at least four expressions; 1 mark for correct substitution of $n = 4$ into at least two expressions]
    b)
n^2 (odd)	$(n + 1)^2$ (even)	$(n - 1)^2$ (even)
$1 + n^2$ (even)	$n^2 - 1$ (even)	$2 + n^2$ (odd)

    n^2 and $2 + n^2$ [3]
    [2 marks for correct identification (odd or even) of at least four expressions; 1 mark for correct identification (odd or even) of at least two expressions]

2. a) New total price is £120 $\times$ 1.05 = £126 [1]
    New mean price is £126 $\div$ 3 [1]
    = £42 [1]
    b) Shirt sale price is £28 $\times$ 0.9 = £25.20
    Trousers sale price = £42 $\times$ 0.8 = £33.60
    He is not correct [3]
    [2 marks for £25.20 and £33.60; 1 mark for £25.20 or £33.60 or a correct multiplier used, i.e. 28 $\times$ 0.9 or 42 $\times$ 0.8]
3. a) $A' \cap B$ [1]
    b) The intersection of A and B [1]
4. a) 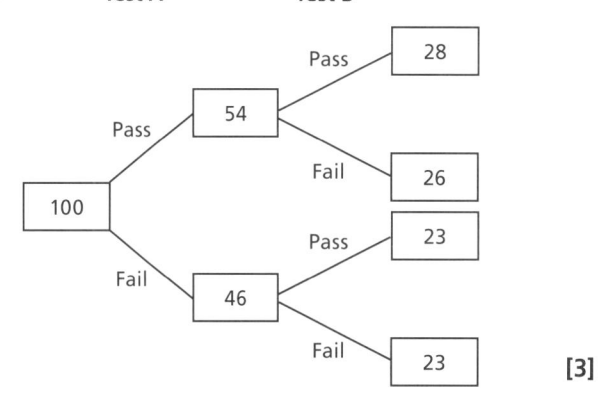
    Tree diagram: 100 → Pass 54 → {Pass 28, Fail 26}; 100 → Fail 46 → {Pass 23, Fail 23} [3]
    [1 mark for each correct pair of branches]
    b) 3 [1]
5. a) 30% of 60 $= \frac{3}{10} \times 60 = 18$ (grey) [1]
    $60 - 18 = 42$
    50% of 42 = 21 (red) [1]
    21 not coloured, so percentage not coloured
    $= \frac{21}{60} \times 100 = 35\%$ [1]
    b) 9 grey and 14 red on outside edge, so $18 + 21 - (9 + 14)$ or $9 + 7 = 16$ coloured and not on outside edge [1]
    So $\frac{16}{60} = \frac{4}{15}$ [1]
6.
Equation	Graph
$y = x^2 + 3x + 2$	C
$y = 2x^3$	E
$y = -2x - 3$	D
$y = \frac{3}{x}$	A
$y = x + 3$	B

    [3]
    [2 marks for at least three correct; 1 mark for at least two correct]
7. Box plot from 112 to 147 with quartiles 123, 132, 137 on Length (cm) axis [3]
    [1 mark for lower quartile (123) or median (132); 1 mark for at least three correctly plotted values from 112, 123, 132, 137, 147]
8. 50 is missing from the frequency scale [1]
    Incorrect point (100, 15) [1]

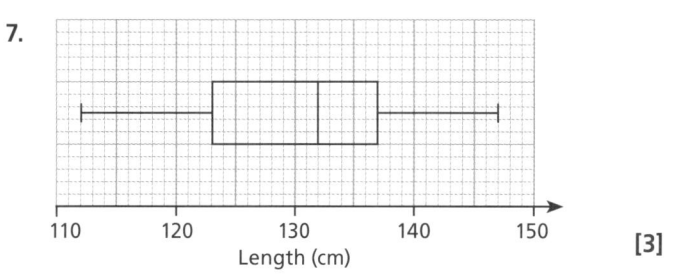

9. a) $(2\sqrt{3})^2 = 2^2 \times (\sqrt{3})^2 = 4 \times 3 = 12$ [1]
   b) $\frac{4}{\sqrt{2}} = \frac{4\sqrt{2}}{\sqrt{2} \times \sqrt{2}} = \frac{4\sqrt{2}}{2} = 2\sqrt{2}$ [1]
      $\sqrt{32} = \sqrt{16 \times 2} = \sqrt{16} \times \sqrt{2} = 4\sqrt{2}$ [1]
      $\frac{4}{\sqrt{2}} + \sqrt{32} = 2\sqrt{2} + 4\sqrt{2} = 6\sqrt{2}$ [1]

10. a) Area of triangle $= \frac{1}{2} \times 9 \times 8 \sin 30°$ [1]
      $= \frac{1}{2} \times 9 \times 8 \times \frac{1}{2} = 18\,cm^2$ [1]
    b) Area of circle $= \frac{3}{2} \times 18 = 27\,cm^2$ [1]
       $\pi r^2 = 27$, $r^2 = \frac{27}{\pi}$ or $r = \sqrt{\frac{27}{\pi}}$ [1]
       $r = 2.93...$, so $r = 2.9\,cm$ (to 1 d.p.) [1]

11. a) $(x-4) - (x+1) = 3(x+1)(x-4)$ [1]
       $x - 4 - x - 1 = 3(x^2 - 3x - 4)$
       or $x - 4 - x - 1 = (3x + 3)(x - 4)$
       or $x - 4 - x - 1 = (x + 1)(3x - 12)$ [2]
       [1 mark for each side]
       $-5 = 3x^2 - 9x - 12$ and $0 = 3x^2 - 9x - 7$ [1]
    b) $x = \frac{-(-9) \pm \sqrt{(-9)^2 - 4(3)(-7)}}{2 \times 3}$ [1]
       $x = \frac{9 \pm \sqrt{81 + 84}}{6} = \frac{9 \pm \sqrt{165}}{6}$ [1]
       $x = 3.64$ or $x = -0.64$ (to 2 d.p.) [1]

12. a) $\vec{QR} = \vec{QS} + \vec{SR}$
       $= 9\mathbf{a} + 6\mathbf{b}$ [1]
    b) Trapezium as $\vec{QR}$ is a multiple of $3\mathbf{a} + 2\mathbf{b}$, so they are parallel [1]

13. a) $72 + 11 + 46 = 129$ [1]
    b) $\frac{72 + 11}{129 + 217} = \frac{83}{346}$ [1]
    c) $\frac{11}{11 + 46} = \frac{11}{57}$ [1]

14. 160 [3]
    [1 mark for $\frac{6}{40}$ or $\frac{24}{6}$ or $\frac{40}{6}$ or $\frac{6}{24}$;
    2 marks for $\frac{6}{40} = \frac{24}{n}$ or $\frac{6}{24} = \frac{40}{n}$]

15. Area of ellipse $= \frac{\pi \times 14 \times 6}{4} = 21\pi\,cm^2$ [1]
    Area of circle $= \pi \times 7^2 = 49\pi\,cm^2$ [1]
    Shaded area $= 49\pi - 21\pi = 28\pi\,cm^2$ [1]

16. Final two lines of working should say
    $= 6m^3 + 21m^2 - 26m^2 - 91m - 20m - 70$
    $= 6m^3 - 5m^2 - 111m - 70$ [2]
    [1 mark for identifying '-70' or that $-91m - 20m = -111m$]

Acknowledgements

The authors and publisher are grateful to the copyright holders for permission to use quoted materials and images.
Every effort has been made to trace copyright holders and obtain their permission for the use of copyright material. The authors and publisher will gladly receive information enabling them to rectify any error or omission in subsequent editions. All facts are correct at time of going to press.

All images ©Shutterstock and HarperCollins*Publishers*

Published by Collins
An imprint of HarperCollins*Publishers* Limited
1 London Bridge Street
London SE1 9GF

HarperCollins*Publishers*
Macken House
39/40 Mayor Street Upper
Dublin 1
D01 C9W8
Ireland

© HarperCollins*Publishers* Limited 2023

ISBN 978-0-00-864743-8

First published 2023

10 9 8 7 6 5 4 3 2 1

All rights reserved. No part of this publication may be reproduced, stored in a retrieval system, or transmitted,
in any form or by any means, electronic, mechanical, photocopying, recording or otherwise, without the prior permission of Collins.

British Library Cataloguing in Publication Data.

A CIP record of this book is available from the British Library.
Publisher: Katie Sergeant
Authors: Trevor Senior, Anne Stothers and Leisa Bovey
Commissioning and Project Management: Richard Toms
Inside Concept Design: Ian Wrigley and Sarah Duxbury
Layout: Ian Wrigley and Contentra Technologies
Cover Design: Sarah Duxbury
Production: Bethany Brohm
Printed in the United Kingdom by Martins the Printers

This book contains FSC™ certified paper and other controlled sources to ensure responsible forest management.

For more information visit: www.harpercollins.co.uk/green